KT-434-423

# HOW TO WIN
# as a
# Mature
# Student

# HOW TO WIN as a Mature Student

Teresa Rickards

First published in 1992



Kogan Page Limited
120 Pentonville Road
London N1 9JN



**British Library Cataloguing in Publication Data**

A CIP record for this book is available from the British Library.

ISBN 0 7494 0677 1

Typeset by DP Photosetting, Aylesbury, Bucks
Printed and bound in Great Britain by
Clays Ltd, St Ives plc

# CONTENTS

# ACKNOWLEDGEMENTS

The author would like to thank Kay Smith, Anna Raynes, Glenna Sutcliffe, Val Butcher, Jean Kelly, Sally Boyd and Dr. Lily Segerman-Peck for their teaching, ideas and advice, which have contributed so much to the background thinking of this book. Many thanks also to Helen Carley for editing help, Rosie Vane-Wright for providing the illustrations, and Jenny Blenkharn for word-processing the manuscript.

The author and publishers would like to express their thanks for permission to include the following illustrations:

Figures 3.1, 3.2 and 3.3 from *NVQs: Standards and Competence* (Kogan Page, 1991) by kind permission of Shirley Fletcher; Figure 3.4 from *APL: A Practical Guide for Professionals* (Kogan Page, 1991) by kind permission of Susan Simosko; Figure 7.1 from *Build your own Rainbow: A Workbook for Career and Life Management* by Barrie Hopson and Mike Scally, Life skills Communications, with acknowledgement to the authors and to Mercury Books.

# FOREWORD

This book is designed to help students with the personal, practical and academic aspects of returning to study after any kind of break.

It begins by asking the reader to explore why they want to return to study, then helps them choose the kind of course most suitable for their needs. The central section on study skills is directed mainly at people entering higher education but is straightforward enough to be accessible to students at any level. The section on time, stress and crisis management will be of help to anyone, whatever their life, study or career plans. The final section helps students to move themselves on towards the world of work, whether they are returning after a career break or seeking career restructuring with improved qualifications after early retirement or redundancy.

The units in each section are linked, but can be read independently in any order. The reader is invited to do some exercises at the end of each unit to check their understanding of the main points and the personal application of those points.

At the point of going to press polytechnics throughout the country are about to be designated as universities and renamed. As some of them are still in the process of receiving Privy Council approval for the changes involved, we have decided to continue to refer to these institutions as polytechnics and would ask the reader to make the necessary adjustment at the time of reading.

# INTRODUCTION

Mature people do not arrive at the threshold of studenthood free of obligations and commitments. A higher education study block at college, polytechnic or university takes a minimum of three to four years, during which the adult student on a grant will be out of the employment market and its prospects. How worthwhile will their prospects be in four or five years time? Will the sacrifice be worth it?

However supportive spouse and family agree to be, do they realise the practical implications of having their husband/wife/mother/father heavily committed to a study schedule on a student grant? Can the situation be financially managed by shared commitment? What are the stresses on family relationships when a leading member is not only practically absent on a regular basis, but needs to be allowed to be mentally absent within the home when the study workload is heavy?

If, as a mature student, you decide to take the plunge, what is the best course of study, what are the entry requirements and how do you go about getting a place? If survival on a grant is prohibitive, what about a part-time degree course with the Open University, or one of the many distance-learning or flexi-study arrangements available all over the country?

As a student, do you know why you want to do this course, what your short-term year-by-year objectives need to be, and what your long-term life and career aims are?

What strategies of contract-setting will you need to have with your family and friends, your tutors and yourself? What sources of personal support can you build up through networks of people you can talk to regularly and contact in a crisis?

What study skills will you need, to make and learn from lecture notes, to express your ideas clearly and effectively in written essays and at oral seminars, to revise for and pass exams, and to access information resources for assignments and research projects?

You will have problems in balancing energy output against recreational input. Time and stress management will need to be part of your planned study strategy, and you will need to have enough personality reserves to survive any personal crises and educational pressure points.

When you have achieved your aim, what happens after the initial euphoria? How will you come to terms with renewed expectations, higher aspirations, changed relationships and the personal growth and self-realisation that accompany the major life transition of high-level academic attainment?

These 20 units will help you to prepare for, begin, develop and advance towards your achievement.

# 1
# STARTING OUT

## UNIT 1. Exploring Prospects

Anyone who sets out to embark on a study programme needs to decide exactly what they want to study, how they intend to do it, how deeply involved they want to get, and how long they want it to go on for. It is also very important to know why you want to study whatever you want to study, and what effect you see it having on your life, not just now or over the next few years, but in the long-term, as a personal and financial investment in your own future over the next 20, 30 or 40 years. Education is a priceless commodity that you cannot buy or acquire by any means other than working and living through it, and in the process of working and living through it you change mentally and in personality into a different kind of person; into someone who can and does rather than someone who could have but didn't.

### Why get involved in study?

Research into motivation shows that people have a hierarchy of needs which are essential to personal survival and a sense of worth and fulfilment in life (Figure 1.1). We all start at levels 1 and 2 down at the bottom of the hierarchy pyramid with our needs for enough to eat and drink, physical safety, and freedom from fear and danger. For very young babies this is enough, but gradually a person begins to emerge who acquires self-respect and a self-image from the affection and regard of the people who initially look after them, and later from the recognition and appreciation of friends, colleagues, teachers and other people in society whose good opinion they value. This is what is happening at Levels 3 and 4, and it goes on happening throughout life as long as Level 1 and 2 needs are being adequately met.

Level 5 is the kind of development someone moves on to when they really start to feel fully an individual, with a sense of self-confidence and self-worth that is no longer damaged by the withdrawal of other people's conditional

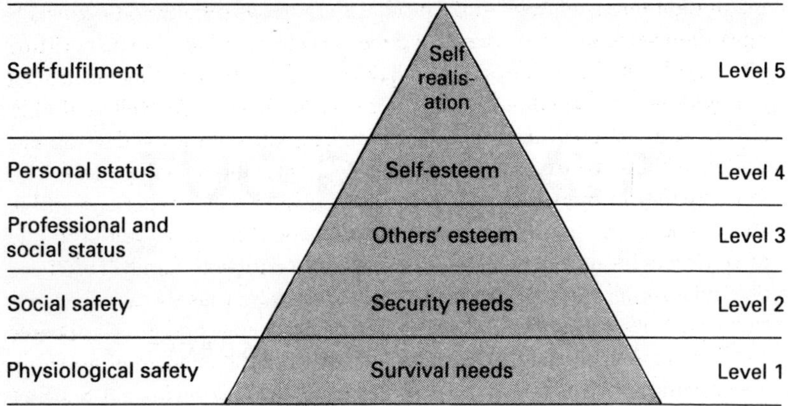


**Figure 1.1** *Maslow hierarchy of needs*

approval. The Level 5 person feels free to be themself and believes that what they have to offer to life, society and other people is their own uniquely worthwhile contribution. People do not develop at Level 5 unless they are very assured at Levels 3 and 4, and they cannot progress or function at Levels 3 and 4 unless Level 1 and 2 needs are being met. As people, we are helped to develop as individuals by our parents, family, friends, teachers and colleagues. As parents, relatives, friends, teachers and colleagues ourselves, we in turn help other people to develop.

What do we need in order to get through the needs hierarchy, or to help other people get through it? At Levels 1 and 2 we just need enough money, though babies and children also need affection and attention or they do not thrive. As we grow up we need a worthwhile and interesting job and way of life, a range of friends who are affirmative and supportive and, for many people, our own stable relationship and, possibly, children. This needs much more than just money, because the way we make the essential money is so very important. We need well-developed and flexible career skills, appropriate professional training and work experience, and the right qualifications and educational background for the job we want and the career we intend to follow. This is why everyone needs a good background education with which to start life and the right level of professional and vocational training to enable them to move on into the field of work they want.

## What's in it for me?

Education is an essential part of the process of self-development and maturation into adulthood. It can lead us to more personally and financially rewarding work with a progressive career structure, rather than just drifting into any old job that comes along and, nowadays, so often getting pushed out of it without any idea of where to go or what to do next. As well as all this, anyone who matures and develops as a student will mature and develop as a person at the same time. They will become a more interesting person, with more to offer to friendships and relationships and a wider experience of life and people to draw on. The combination of financial and social gains can lead to a different lifestyle for you, for your partner, and for your family if you have one. Education has to go on throughout our lives, not just because our jobs change but because our lives change; because we change and grow as people and need new skills and new knowledge to meet the challenges of growing-up, growing successful, growing wiser and, eventually, growing old. Some of the most successful students are those who come to study for the first time at retirement, because they bring with them so much and have so much to offer.

## Who can help me to choose?

You may already know what you want or need to study, in which case you need to find out where it is on offer in your area. The alternatives to studying at a college, polytechnic or university in your district are either going away to live and study for the duration of your course, or studying at home by distance-learning or flexi-study. If you are eligible for a mature student grant, you could possibly consider living away from home during term times, but this would depend on family and financial commitments. If you need to continue working full-time while you study, supported correspondence study through the Open University or the National Extension College, or a part-time degree through your nearest university, are routes that have been taken by many mature people.

The addresses of the most important national distance-learning organizations are given at the end of this book; they will provide details of the broad range of home-study programmes they offer, with costs and arrangements.

Maybe you are one of the people who realises that they need to do some study to improve their qualifications but doesn't feel sure quite what. Perhaps the first question you should ask yourself is why you need to study. Have you been made redundant or retired early from one job, and do you need to make a future in something quite different? Do you want to return to work after a career break of several years, and need old work skills updating, or training in completely new work skills? Are you a person in their twenties who has realised that most jobs come to a dead end where promotion prospects finish unless a worker can offer additional qualifications?

If you are a person in any of these situations you need the maximum amount of careers advice you can get, from your local careers service and from any other educational guidance agencies there are in your area. If you are registered as unemployed, government-sponsored local centres throughout the country offer courses of retraining in new work skills, and preparatory courses and advice on becoming self-employed. It is difficult for an adviser to help when the client has no idea what they want, so, when you go for your guidance interview, do have some tentative ideas to start thinking about, even if you find that you have to change your mind as better ideas emerge. There are several very good guide books for mature people returning to work and study (see the Additional Reading section at the end of this book) which are obtainable through public libraries, if not already available there for reference. They can help you to think about what is available, to decide what you are interested in following up, and to consider what qualifications and skills you already have to transfer to your new field of work and study.

Colleges, polytechnics and universities will provide prospectuses of the courses they offer, and you will need to contact the tutor responsible for student admissions to the course you want for details of the entry qualifications and to make an application. Gaining admission to a longer, higher-level academic course takes time. Application to a university, polytechnic or higher education college for a degree course needs to be made a year in advance, and further education colleges welcome applications as far in advance of the beginning of the academic year as possible, particularly if you want to be sure of a place on a popular course. Part-time day and evening classes at local colleges do try to cater for local people's needs and will arrange admission at short notice if possible, but there can be problems on practical skills courses, such as computing and word-processing, where the use of available equipment dictates limits on the number of students who can be admitted.

## What will it all cost?

You need to think not just about money but about time, effort and commitment. Whatever study course you take, you will need to attend classes regularly and be prepared to do some homework and background reading at home. For a practically-based course, such as computing or word-processing, there may be less homework, but there will need to be many hours of practice on the machines to gain proficiency and, increasingly, people who intend to work in these skills areas are buying their own machines to gain the additional practice at home.

If you are doing several hours part-time day or evening study, you can expect to do at least as many hours again in study outside the classroom, at home or in the library. This is particularly so today, when many courses are continually assessed on the basis of assignments written by students throughout the year, rather than on a single pass or fail examination at the end of the course. The schedule is tough to keep up with, and does require constant effort and commitment, but the student collects marks towards the final result as they go along and is aware of their progress all the time.

Most courses leading to a professional qualification take more than one year, and degree courses take three to four years full-time, and even longer part-time. This means that whatever effort it has cost you to get through just one year has to be repeated again and again until the course is finished. These courses take considerable commitment in time and in mental and nervous stamina, and you need to be physically and mentally fit and energetic, as well as emotionally stable, to complete the heavy study schedule involved.

You also have to accept that there are sacrifices to be made. Time, energy and money have to be invested in education, and hobbies and interests that usually take up a lot of these may have to be severely rationed. You may have to say good-bye, temporarily or even permanently, to friends who no longer share your ideals, and to look for others who do.

## What are the long-term gains?

Modern principles of educational and careers guidance include the idea of personal careership; the idea that a person should decide at the outset of his or her adult life what their objectives are in the short, medium and long term, and what strategies they need to adopt to attain them. Educational institutions and work organisations are moving towards the idea of work and study credits and records of achievement, so that a young person can start out with clear evidence of what their study attainments and practical competences are, and have a record of transferable skills to present to a future employer or educational institution and to build on throughout life.

For most people, future job prospects will demand flexibility, in attitude and competence, and the ability to retrain at intervals throughout working life as current skills become outdated. It is the person who cannot or will not adapt who will find themself unemployable as we enter the next century. Education today needs to be seen as an opportunity to develop the professional and personal skills that we need in order to operate in a changing world, rather than as a body of knowledge that is ours for life and needs neither addition nor review. In order to be confident that we can earn enough money to give us the lifestyle we would like, we shall need to use our skills to adapt to what employment prospects there are, rather than expect life to offer us what we feel we deserve as a reward for our early efforts and achievements. An individual person may end up doing totally different work from what their initial training prepared them for, and needing to change tack several times in a working lifetime in order to remain in work.

The objectives we set ourselves in life need to be clear and specific, but the routes we travel in order to get to them may have to be reviewed and re-decided as our life circumstances change. The goals themselves may alter as time goes on and we review our personal priorities. It is as important to have a statement of our personal objectives in life as it is to have a statement of our career objectives; and we should be prepared to draw up and maintain our own personal records of achievement alongside the ones prepared for us by employers and educational institutions. The long-term gains are that we take charge of our own personal and professional lives instead of just drifting and having no control over where we eventually arrive.

## EXERCISES ON MOTIVATION

**1. Consider your life goals over the next 2, 5, 10 and 20 years under the following headings:**

- **money and lifestyle**
- **career and work**
- **family and friends**
- **personal development**

**Ask yourself how you would like to be, what you would like to do and what you would like to have.**

**Make your goals specific but realistic enough to be attainable. They should have deadlines for achievement based on realistic time spans. They should also be *measurable*; you must be able to know when you've got there. Write down your goals and re-read them regularly.**

**2. The wheel in Figure 1.2 is to help you to decide where you are now. Shade in the parts in proportion to how satisfactory each is now. The wheel should balance, ideally. If it doesn't you can see which parts of your life you need to work on.**

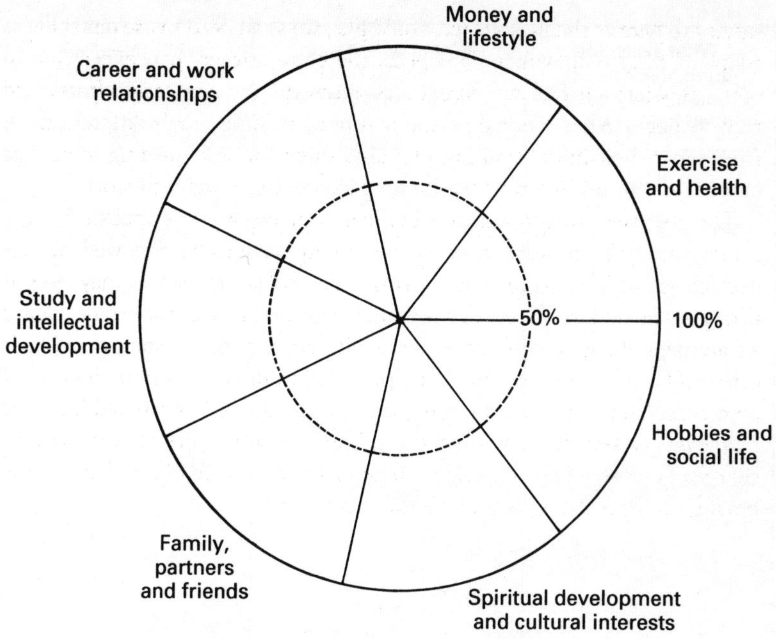


Figure 1.2 *Life balance*

**3. Choose a time in your life, say 2, 5, 10 or 20 years ahead. Write down your career objective as:**

**'I want to reach the position of .................................... in my career in ...... years time'.**

**Write a few sentences saying why you would like this. Now complete the table in Figure 1.3.**

**4. Modern motivational research has advanced from the Maslow hierarchy of needs to take account of what motivates people to work towards change in their lives and careers. They do not just stay where circumstances push them or drift to wherever seems appropriate at the time. People will make the effort to change their lives and careers when they see the outcome of change as attractive to them and feel that they have a realistic chance of success. With this in mind, outline your financial and lifestyle goals as follows:**

| What skills and qualifications do you already have to help you? | What could make you fail to reach your objective? | What skills and qualifications do you need to get to help you? |
|---|---|---|
| | | |

Figure 1.3 *Finding your career objectives*

**'By the time I reach the age of ...., I want to be earning at least .................. in present-day terms. I want sufficient income to ..........................................................................................................'**

**Now complete the table in Figure 1.4.**

**5. Choose one thing you would like to be, have or do as a person. Describe it as specifically as you can.**

**Say *why* you would like to achieve your aim. List the reasons why you could and should achieve it. What obstacles could possibly stand in the way of your achieving it? Decide on one obstacle and how you could tackle it. How will you know when you've achieved what you want?**

| What are you already doing to achieve this goal? | What could make you fail? | What else do you need to begin doing to achieve this goal? |
|---|---|---|
| | | |

**Figure 1.4** *Finding your life objectives*

## UNIT 2. Negotiating Relationships

You can think about this aspect of what you are proposing to do either before or after you look at Units 3 and 4; or preferably before *and* after, as you might need a lot of second thoughts on the problem before you decide how to tackle it. Going back to work or study presents two kinds of problems: the mechanical ones of reorganising daily life so that you have the time and energy to meet the extra commitments you are undertaking, and the intellectual or mental ones of acquiring the new work or study skills that you are going to need to discharge these commitments. If you are returning to work, the skills you need will be job-specific, and if you haven't got them now you will need to get them either in advance or by on-the-job training. If you are returning to study, Units 9, 10, 11 and 12 will be of help to you in getting started.

## In what ways shall I need my family's help?

What I want to look at here is the practical problem of coping with the impact on daily routines and family life that becoming a full-time worker or a full-time student will have. The issues will be the same for someone who is a part-time student, or a distance-learning or flexi-study student; they will just be even more complex and difficult to cope with because your study course will go on for longer, and you will most likely be working full- or part-time as well. I don't want to draw a major distinction between going back to work and going back to study. Taken on full-time, both demand at least an eight-hour working day and a five-day working week, with some evening and weekend work for both the student and the person with a responsible job. The only big difference is that the working person will be generating income while the student will be losing it in various ways, temporarily at least.

Your partner and family will have become used to your being available, if not 24 hours a day then for as many of your waking hours as you are present in the home. If you are out at work during the day, your partner will expect you to deal with those domestic issues and chores that are part of your brief, on your return. If your day is spent caring for the home and, possibly, family, your partner will expect the domestic side of life to have been dealt with while they are at work, and will not expect housework to be going on in the evenings. That is the way things are done in our society; by division of labour, with each partner attending to an agreed area of household and family responsibility. It is probably the most convenient way of doing things for couples with children, but it is insufficiently flexible for modern society.

Whether you are going back to work or going back to study, you will need to operate at a very high level of tight organisation to fit in everything you need to do; but at the same time you will need to be flexible and adaptable enough to reorganise routines and schedules when the unexpected turns up, as it often will. You will also need to set boundaries clearly, so that your partner and family understand that what you are doing is serious and that you are committed to it, and that there will be certain times when you will be at home with work to do, and unavailable for anything other than serious emergencies. Children of any age can be totally inconsiderate of their parents' needs for some freedom as adults, and need to have it made very clear that you will be available for them at certain times, but that you must be left undisturbed at others.

As a prospective returner, whether to study or full- or part-time work, you will need to analyse very carefully just what things you have to do at home, and at work or college, during a day and in the course of a week. Unit 13 on time management is intended to help you to do this, and it might be an idea to work through this sooner rather than later, as it is a surprising experience for most people to see how quite large tracts of time can be frittered away by nothing in particular, and how difficult it is to be 100 per cent accountable for what you have chosen to do with time; even if it's to do nothing. Unit 14 on conserving energy is also important enough to read through early on as well as later, as time and energy will be your most precious commodities in what you are going to undertake. You will not have enough of either to do everything you have been doing up to now, and the answer must lie in some delegation to the people who share your personal life.

## How can I persuade my family to be supportive?

If you are going back to work now, it should be obvious to your family that they will benefit financially immediately and for the foreseeable future. Each partner in a relationship needs to be open with the other about individual income, as well as about joint income available to the family after other commitments have been met. What I mean here is that one or other partner could have children from a previous family to help to maintain, or an older parent who is receiving financial help. Both partners also need to understand what deductions from income are made by employers: such as tax at standard rate, national insurance and superannuation contributions. Married women are now required to complete their own income tax returns and need to be quite clear about how this is done, as it is a legal obligation.

If you have a job now, or are to start one soon, you can work out in salary terms how much extra money is going to be available to the family because of your efforts and what improvements there will be as your career progresses and you gain promotion or move into better jobs. If you are returning to study full-time, the idea is the same, but there will be a delay of up to five years while you gain your qualification and then move back into the workforce and start to generate income again. If you know what kind of job you are aiming for, you can find out the salary level now and, adding 5 per cent per year over the next five years, you can arrive at an estimate of what you will be earning then. These are the kinds of facts and figures that can persuade the unconvinced that your going back to work or study is a good idea. If it's back to study you need to offset the cost against the long-term gains, and we will look at this in Unit 4.

The idea that I want to stress here is that anyone in the family who will benefit, financially or in any other way, by the fact that you are working now or will be doing so in the future, should be willing to share in the effort of making that possible. If your existing family income is high enough for your financial contribution not to be crucial, you still have every reason to see family life as a source of personal happiness and have the right to expect that others in your family will help you to do what contributes to your happiness. No parent or partner is just a domestic support system, a meal-ticket, or the back-up service that enables other people to go off enjoying themselves non-stop. Should you have money to spare, getting as much good, paid domestic help as possible would be one very wise thing to do with some of it.

## How much support is it reasonable to expect?

When you first start to look to your family and friends for support in your new venture, you might at first find they are not very much forthcoming. Before you start to feel annoyed or taken for granted, stop and think just how much real support and interest you have ever given them for anything they have wanted to do, beyond what concerns the basics of your joint life or what you have found convenient. Many partners see each other as mutual solutions to each other's problems, rather than as individual people with lives, hopes and plans of their own. While this is understandable in some ways, when much that is personal has to be put aside while children are brought up, it will not do as the continuing basis for a long-term relationship, as children grow up and leave home, leaving the parental couple to face their future together.

Good relationship support has to be mutual, and there has to be an appreciation that, however close people are, there will be areas of privacy and difference that have to be allowed for. The other major thing that has to be allowed for is change over time. Though we remain basically the same people, our personalities develop continuously throughout life and our tastes and interests can change so much that others can almost see us as having become different people. Good relationships with partners and friends need enough flexibility to allow for this and a good enough level of communication to maintain awareness of what is going on. Our children above all need us to take this kind of approach in our relationships with them, as they more than anybody else change drastically and almost unrecognisably in the time during which we know them.

Quality in relationships is something that I shall emphasise again and again in the course of this book, as it needs to be searched for and worked on throughout life. It doesn't just happen, unless you are very, very lucky, but there are ways of getting it. It may not be realistic to expect a spouse or partner to totally understand why you need work or educational development for your own sense of fulfilment. They may not see the need for it in your joint situation. You probably do not fully understand what they find fulfilling in their work and interests. You may not ever have felt it was your concern to think about it, and yet you may experience disappointment with your relationship when the interest you now need, but have never given, is not forthcoming for you and your plans.

## EXERCISES ON MANAGING RELATIONSHIPS

**I'm stepping ahead of myself here, by using the ideas of practical competences that are introduced in Unit 3. If you are reading this unit after Units 3 and 4, this approach will already be familiar to you. If not, it doesn't matter, as the basic ideas needed at this point are quite simple, but it would help if you would glance forward to Figure 4.1 in Unit 4 so that you understand which competences I am**

| Unit of competence | PERFORMANCE CRITERIA |
|---|---|
| **Unit of competence 4:** Domestic management of self and others | Eat nutritious meals |
| | Keep household jobs under control |
| | Keep self and family organised |
| | |
| | |
| | |
| | |

Figure 2.1 *Domestic management* (Exercise 1)

**referring to. I would like to introduce student competences 4 and 5 at this point, and to ask you to think about them in relation to domestic management of yourself and your family and the management of personal relationships in general. I want to emphasise the skills of negotiation, cooperation, appreciation and assertion in dealing with all the relationships you need to manage in your life, whether they are part of personal, social, working or student life.**

1. **The *unit of competence* says what the overall aim to be achieved is. It can be broken down into *elements of competence*, such as shopping, cooking, washing, ironing, cleaning, gardening, home maintenance, car maintenance, DIY and so on. The *performance criteria* are ways in which you can see that the *elements of competence* have worked successfully and made their individual contributions to the overall aim of the *unit of competence*. *Elements of competence* are abilities whereas *performance criteria* are specific achievements. Please do your own break-down of**

| Unit of competence | PERFORMANCE CRITERIA |
|---|---|
| **Unit of competence 5:** Managing personal relationships | Get on with partner |
| | Get on with children |
| | Get on with family |
| | Get on with neighbours |
| | Get on with existing friends |
| | Get on with new friends |
| | |
| | |
| | |

Figure 2.2 *Personal relationship management* (Exercise 2)

**essential household tasks and write in as many *performance criteria* as you need. Each *performance criterion* shows that you have actually done, and regularly do, exactly what it says. Don't bother about budgeting money. That's coming in Unit 4.**

2. **The *unit of competence* gives the overall aim, and again I have merged *elements of competence* with *performance criteria* for simplicity. Please add more of your own if you belong to a church or social community or have contacts with any special interest groups outside work. 'Getting on' here means having time for people and being on good terms with them, as far as is appropriate and possible. The key skills needed are negotiation, or working towards what you want from someone else; cooperation, or giving some of your own ground in order to get it; appreciation, or showing you value what the other person has done towards giving you what you want; and assertion, or staking a claim firmly to what you know is rightfully yours when other people don't seem to realise that it is.**

## UNIT 3. Acquiring Competence

Units 3 and 4 are linked and belong together. How much of each you need to be aware of depends on where you see yourself arriving in about five years' time. If you want to return to work as soon as possible and already know the career direction you want to take, Unit 3 guides you through the new system of National Vocational Qualifications, which is what you can expect to confront in one form or another if you move back into the business, commercial or vocational work scene and want to have your prior work experience accredited. Unit 4 moves further on, for anyone who wants to enter higher education in order to obtain a degree or diploma through university, polytechnic or Open University study, whether full- or part-time. This requires a different way of accrediting prior learning, but the stages the student needs to go through are in principle the same. Both Units 3 and 4 contain ideas that will be of help and interest to both groups of people.

### What is APL and why?

Accreditation of prior learning (APL) is not a new idea. Some kind of APL has always been carried out at important transition points in the education system. All tests and examinations that determine whether or not children and teenagers can be awarded a particular qualification, or whether or not they can proceed to the next stage of the system, are ways of accrediting prior learning. Certificates and test results are just ways of saying what a young person, or indeed an older person, can reasonably be expected to know about a particular subject or skill area. Prior learning is what you already know how to do, and accreditation is finding an appropriate way to give you credit for it. If you are moving into college or university study, your future teachers need to know where you are now. If you are moving into work, your future employers need to know what they can rely on you to do.

In the past in England and Wales, testing of children at age 11+ was used to decide what kind of secondary school children should go to. Examinations such as the General Certificate of Education (GCE), or its modern replacement the General Certificate of Secondary Education (GCSE), have been used very widely as school-leaving qualifications. Passes at the ordinary level (GCE 'O' level) attained at age 16 gave employers a means of deciding whether or not to appoint a young person to their first job, and gave further education college teachers a way of deciding what kind of part-time study course would be suitable for them. Passes at the advanced level (GCE 'A' level) were obtained at age 18 or 19, usually after a further two to three years study at school but also by part-time day and evening study for young people who were working. They were used, as they still are, as the decisive factor in awarding a young person a higher education or university student place. The Scottish education system has always been different, and Scotland has led the way in modern methods of implementing APL in the United Kingdom.

While the emphasis in the past was almost entirely on children and young people as the ones who most needed to benefit from education, the need of modern society for a well-qualified and flexible workforce has become inescapably obvious. People who qualified and obtained their work skills more than a few years ago need them up-dating. Women who dropped out of work to have a family need re-skilling, as do many men who have had to face redundancy and prolonged unemployment. Almost no one can now expect to go through a working life without making changes and developing new skills; and as good jobs become fewer the competition for them increases. The keys to survival and success in this kind of working environment are training to high standards with appropriate recognition, and personal flexibility in adapting to new work situations with their demands for new skills and new knowledge.

What people carry with them throughout life, and bring to every new work and life situation, is their own experience, from every source; and an array of skills which are either transferable directly or adaptable with re-training. The thinking behind APL is that recognition of much that people take for granted should be made official, so that skills and knowledge acquired outside the formal education system can be used by the person to move back into the system beyond the level of a complete beginner, thus saving them, and their employer if they have one, time and money. For people who have been unwaged for some time, such as family women at home and unemployed people generally, the idea of crediting unpaid work is seen as crucial to their progress. All domestic work, community work and voluntary work requires specific skills to be carried out efficiently. So does the kind of household maintenance and DIY work that most people do routinely or as a hobby. The brief of APL has been to establish formal standards by which these skills can be recognised and accredited to the people who already have them.

## What are NVQs and who can get them?

The 1986 government white paper *Working Together - Education and Training*, laid the groundwork for the introduction of APL into education and training in England and Wales:

> Qualifications and standards are not luxuries. They are necessities, central to securing a competent and adaptable workforce. Economic performance and individual job satisfaction both depend on maintaining and improving standards of competence.

This same white paper established the National Council for Vocational Qualifications (NCVQ) whose task was to re-organise the ways in which traditional vocational courses were structured and the ways in which their end qualifications were awarded. The two main changes which NCVQ recommended and moved to implement were the restructuring of traditional courses along unit-by-unit or modular lines, and the replacement of traditional examinations with a method of unit-by-unit assessment leading to a final accreditation based on practical competences.

The word 'competence' means that someone is capable of doing something effectively. Competence, as used in NCVQ discussions, refers specifically to work-related skills and the ability to perform activities within an occupation. It also has broader implications, such as the ability to transfer skills and knowledge to new situations within the occupational area, and ultimately to completely new areas of work, should job flexibility require it during a person's working life. The government Training Agency in their 1988/89 document further recognized and drew attention to the personal aspects of work competence:

> It encompasses organisation and planning of work, innovation and coping with non-routine activities. It includes those qualities of personal effectiveness that are required in the workplace to deal with co-workers, managers and customers.

It is these qualities of personal competence, as well as the work-related ones, that I shall return to in detail when we consider the personal qualities you are going to need to succeed as a mature student.

The result of NCVQ's work over the last few years has been to put in place, in adult and further education colleges throughout the country, a system of learning and a process of assessment that lead towards student accreditation in the award of National Vocational Qualifications (NVQs). The emphasis in assessment is on the student showing that they can actually do what is required of them. How and where they have learned to do it is not important. This opens the way to accrediting prior learning for people who have not travelled the conventional educational route and, with the unit-by-unit structure and assessment, it enables people who can already demonstrate their competences to short-cut parts of a course that they do not need to repeat, and to move ahead on a faster track towards the NVQ objectives they want to reach.

The way of thinking about an NVQ accreditation is to break down a worker's skill requirements into basic **units of competence**, and to further break these down into *elements of competence*. To show that you have these

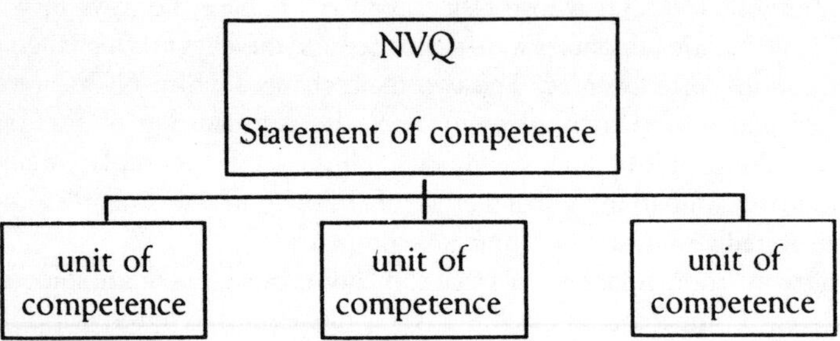


*NVQs are not linked to any specified course of study, nor are they time-based; candidates achieve units at their own pace, the primary form of assessment is observation of performance in the workplace and there are no restrictions of age, previous qualifications etc., regarding access to assessment.*

**Figure 3.1** *Unit-based structure*

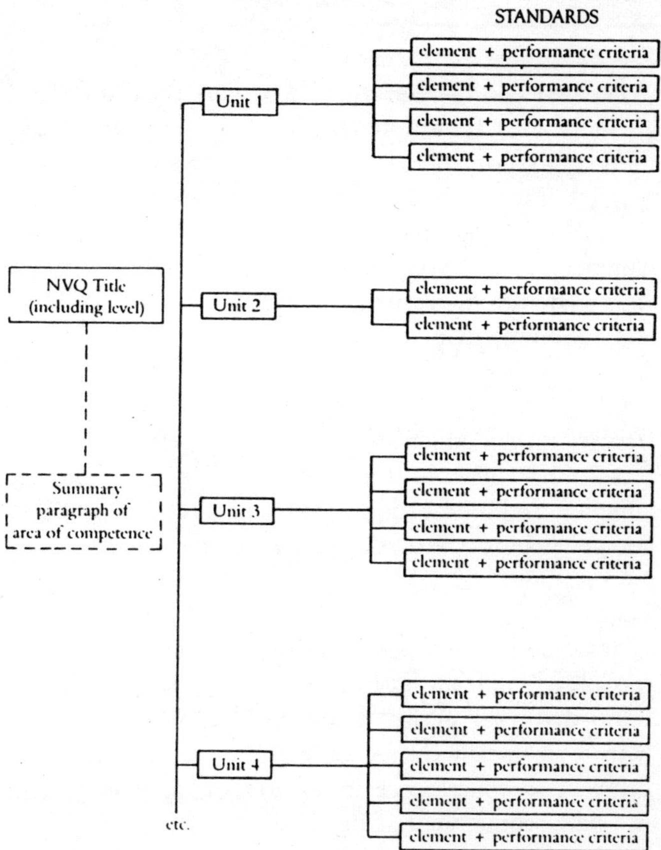


Figure 3.2 *NVQ structure*

competences you have to meet precise *performance criteria.* From knowing what an employer will want you to do, you need to move to the stage of showing that you can do it. Figures 3.1 and 3.2 show the plan on paper for building up the competences that can lead to an NCVQ-accredited award.

The first work and training areas to be thought through completely in NVQ competence terms have been the practical ones, such as hairdressing, engineering and business administration; but NVQ competence criteria are now being applied to areas such as social work and vocational and personal counselling, where interpersonal skills are such a strong component of

*Level 1*
Competence in the performance of work activities which are in the main routine and predictable or provide a broad foundation, primarily as a basis for progression.

*Level 2*
Competence in a broader and more demanding range of work activities involving greater individual responsibility and autonomy than at level 1.

*Level 3*
Competence in skilled areas that involve performance of a broad range of work activities, including many that are complex and non-routine. In some areas, supervisory competence may be a requirement at this level.

*Level 4*
Competence in the performance of complex, technical, specialised and professional work activities, including those involving design, planning and problem-solving, with a significant degree of personal accountability. In many areas competence in supervision or management will be a requirement at this level.

**Figure** 3.3 *NVQ framework – level descriptors*

professional and personal effectiveness. NVQs will eventually lead to nationally recognised occupational standards being applied in all areas of work, and ultimately, it is intended, to recognition for job mobility purposes throughout the European Community.

At present there are 4 levels at which NCVQ gives accreditation beginning at the most basic level of job training (NVQ1) and leading to the stage at which the person can take on work with a considerable degree of personal accountability both for themself and others (NVQ4). The official description of levels within the NVQ framework is shown in Figure 3.3. It is envisaged at present that NVQ3 will be the level at which international accreditation of compatibility will begin to be established in the future. It is important to realise that NCVQ is not itself the body that awards vocational qualifications. What it does is to accredit the qualifications awarded by other bodies when these meet its officially published standards and detailed criteria, and to add the official NCVQ seal of approval to the awarding body's certificate, which becomes the student's record of achievement.

By 1993 a national funding council should be in place to work out in detail how APL can work for individual returners to work and study who have not followed one of the NVQ-accredited courses leading to an award from a national examining body. At present APL is being widely used to fast-track mature returners to a later stage of an existing course. The hope for the future is that it may be possible, with very careful counsellor-to-student APL, and a combination of flexi-study and occasional skills workshops, to get a student to the point of NVQ accreditation without their having to attend an official college course at all. This is the ultimate aim for all levels of student access up to university and polytechnic entrance.

## What can you expect when you try to get APL?

As a potential student customer of whatever college, polytechnic or university you are applying to, you need to think not only of how the system is going to process you, but also of what you have the right to expect. Someone, somewhere is paying for your student place in the institution, or for the tutorial attention you get as a distance-learning or flexi-study student. If it is not you, then your sponsoring body, or whoever is footing the bill, has the right to expect efficiency and accountability from the institution and the people delivering its services to the public. It is a two-way process. You have expectations of them and there are expectations that they have the right to have of you. Counselling, assessment and tutorial staff are the only people who can not just put you on the right track, but help you to keep yourself on the right track. Figure 3.4 shows the stages you will need to go through to get APL, whatever you want to do.

*Pre-entry* is, on the part of the college, the work they do through publicity and marketing, to attract you as a student customer. On your part it is, or should be, the careful thinking through of why, as well as what, you want to study. This means looking at not only your work objectives, but your life objectives, personal and social as well as financial.

*Candidate profiling* and *gathering of evidence* I am placing together, as

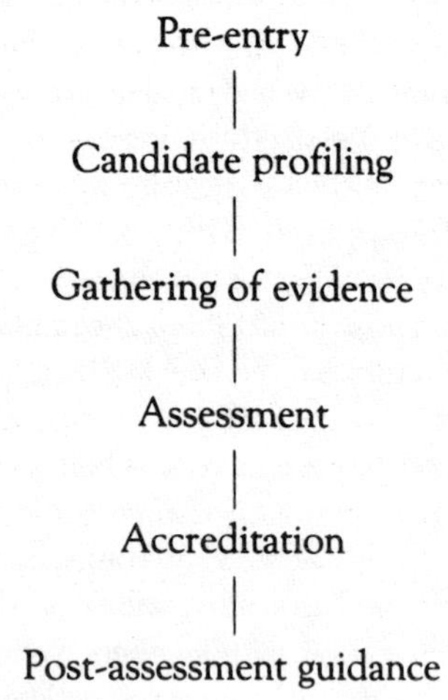


Figure 3.4 *The six stages of the APL model*

many institutions do, since they are just different ways of doing the same thing. If you are a prospective NVQ candidate, these stages will be crucial for you. It is your job to compile a *portfolio of evidence* in support of whatever claim to having a skill you want to make. You will need *direct* evidence, in the form of practical things that you can do or make, to show to an assessor. These could range from letters you have typed or word-processed, cakes or clothes you have made, examples of DIY projects you have carried out at home, to written assignments from previous study courses. You will also be greatly helped by any *indirect* evidence, in the form of certificates or qualifications awarded for previous courses of study or training, or letters of validation from previous employers, that you can offer an assessor to show that other responsible people have found you competent in the ways you want to claim.

As an NVQ candidate you will receive the advice and help you need to put together this portfolio of evidence at a fairly long initial interview with a general counsellor. For some colleges this is part of the pre-entry stage of the process, and it gives the counsellor the opportunity to decide how realistic you are being about the level of skill you can demonstrate that you already have. It is counter-productive in the long run for the people doing this initial counselling to let you think you are ready for assessment when you aren't.

This is also the stage at which the counsellor will explore in detail your previous history and the transferable skills you are bringing in from unpaid voluntary, community, or household work and from other jobs.

*Assessment* and *accreditation* I will also place together, as they are continuous stages of the process by which the educational system dealing with you will move you forward. When your portfolio of evidence or skills profile is ready, the general counsellor will move you on to an assessor. It is the job of the assessor to decide whether or not the evidence you are presenting in support of your claim to a particular skill is enough. They may also test you on the skill you claim, both practically and by direct questioning. What they are trying to do is to see if you meet the performance criteria for a specific element of work or study competence, as shown in Figure 3.2. If you can show competence in a number of work-related skills, you will then have what is called a 'skills profile', and your elements of competence may together add up to a unit of competence, as indeed they should eventually.

An external verifier is someone from outside the college who represents the examining or awarding body, and they will be invited to see you and your portfolio of work on their next visit to the college. The external verifier is the person who says 'Yes' or 'No', to your assessor's opinion. If the external verifier says 'Yes', you can then be given official accreditation of competence and be ready to move on to the next stage of Figure 3.4. If he or she says 'No', you will be assessed as not yet competent and be given further advice on how to strengthen your portfolio or skills profile in support of your claim. It would be unusual for an external verifier not to confirm the opinion of an experienced assessor, but they do have the final decision and, again, it is not in your interests to try to run before you can walk.

The last stage shown in Figure 3.4 is *post-assessment guidance*. This will be given to you by your assessor, with some consultation with your general counsellor. You may be advised to further develop your skills profile by planning to work towards meeting the performance criteria for another range of elements of competence; so building up another unit of competence towards your objective of an NVQ accreditation, the end product shown in Figure 3.2. If you are not quite ready to move on, you will either be advised to join an existing course at a more basic level or, if you prefer a flexi-study or distance-learning arrangement, be given an open-learning package from which you can work at home towards the same objective. It is also possible that your assessor and general counsellor between them may see your talents as lying in a totally different area, and may ask you to think about something completely new.

At present the process of APL, as it is intended to work for the benefit of most mature returners, is not cost-free. It is, at the time of writing, perhaps more expensive than most people could afford, but a broad consensus exists between the main political parties in the UK on the importance of widening access to education and training, and eventually there should be a funding mechanism for giving at least some grant assistance to prospective students in most need. It is possible at present to use APL to move forward on a fast track towards achieving well-established existing qualifications that are NCVQ-validated. The Business and Technician Education Council (BTEC), the London Chamber of Commerce (LCC), the Business Training Council (BTC), the City and Guilds of London Institute (CGLI), the Royal Society of Arts (RSA) and the Pitman Examinations Institute (PEI), all take a positive approach to the aims of NCVQ, as do countless employers nationwide. The matching-up of levels between NVQs and Open College units will also lead along a continuous accreditation route to higher education entry.

## EXERCISES ON TRANSFERABLE SKILLS

**1.a) Write down what you consider your main job to be now, whether paid or unwaged:**
**I am a ..................................................................**
**(eg, housewife/bus driver/teacher/nurse/unemployed or retired person seeking work.)**

**b) Write down what your roles are in your immediate family, extended family and circle of friends:**
**I am a ..................................................................**
**(eg, mother/father/husband/wife/sister/brother/son daughter/close friend/old friend.)**

**c) Write down what your work or helping roles are in your community, whether paid or voluntary:**
**I am a ..................................................................**
**(eg, youth club organiser/hospital or prison visitor/ school governor/local government councillor/charity fund-raiser/ WVS helper/CAB organiser.)**

**2. Think about what you do in your work, family and community roles. Try to analyse the work and management skills you use and rate how good you think you are on the scale below. If you feel self-confident enough, ask a colleague or an honest friend to read through your self-ratings and comment on them.**

**Scale rating: very competent (VC); fairly competent (FC): adequately competent (AC); not yet competent (NYC).**

**I DEAL WITH: a) *My job* (paid or unwaged)**

| I WORK WITH: | HOW COMPETENT AM I? (Ring your self-rating) | | | |
|---|---|---|---|---|
| People | VC | FC | AC | NYC |
| Practical things | VC | FC | AC | NYC |
| Factual information | VC | FC | AC | NYC |
| Numerical information | VC | FC | AC | NYC |
| New ideas | VC | FC | AC | NYC |
| **I MANAGE:** | | | | |
| Time | VC | FC | AC | NYC |
| Money | VC | FC | AC | NYC |
| Arrangements | VC | FC | AC | NYC |
| Relationships | VC | FC | AC | NYC |
| Enough for myself | VC | FC | AC | NYC |

**Repeat this 10-item rating exercise for b) dealing with family and friends, and c) dealing with your community and voluntary work roles.**

**Count up how many times out of 30 you have given yourself VC, FC, AC, or NYC and you will have the beginnings of a profile of transferable skills that you already have and can take with you to any new job or life situation. You will also see which areas of work and life need attention and improvement.**

**If you would like to give yourself a numerical score, make VC=10, FC=7, AC=5 and NYC=3. This will give you a maximum possible score of 300 and you can compare your personal score with this.**

## UNIT 4. Obtaining Access

If you see your future in a career for which you will need a university or polytechnic degree or diploma, you will need to look into how to gain admission to the course you want. If you are not sure what you would like to study, or where you would like to study it, write to the registrar's department of several universities, polytechnics and colleges of higher education and ask them to send you a copy of their current undergraduate prospectus. Reference departments of public libraries carry a range of these prospectuses and they will have available very detailed higher education directories from which you can get addresses and contact names in particular subject departments. The most important ones are given at the end of this book. Don't dismiss the idea of getting a degree as beyond you; it almost certainly isn't. And don't think of having a degree as something unimportant that you needn't bother with. People who don't take the trouble to get a degree when they could constantly have to prove that they are as good as people who have.

## What is access and how can I get it?

If you are a person aged 21 or over, who has not continued straight from full-time education in school or further education college to university, you are classified as a mature student and are eligible to be considered for higher education entrance by the access route. What access does is to take you through the APL stages we looked at in Unit 3 (Figure 3.4), in the way that the particular university, polytechnic or higher education college thinks is appropriate for the course of study you have chosen. Whether you want to become a full-time student or a part-time student will not matter. What access will do is to bring you to the point at which you are competent to undertake advanced study. The practical competences you will need in order to be effective as a mature student we will look at later.

You will need to decide at the *pre-entry* stage whether you should become a full-time or a part-time student from the point of view of cost. Most mature students choose to take the part-time route, rather than give up their job and lose their income. Part-time study does take quite a lot longer, but the higher education system has made itself extremely flexible in order to accommodate the very varied needs of its mature student population. Some students, such as family people with considerable domestic commitments to children or older relatives, prefer the part-time route with its provision for taking a break from study should personal circumstances make it particularly difficult to continue at certain points. If you are fortunate enough to be able to return as a full-time student, you will find yourself welcome and soon at home amongst a younger generation of people who will challenge and stimulate you, and amongst whom you will almost certainly make some permanent friends.

At the *pre-entry* stage it is important to talk to someone in the university, polytechnic or higher education college who can advise you about where you stand now regarding their entry requirements to the degree course you want. The institution's student advisory services will be able to put you in touch with whoever is the mature student adviser for the institution or the admissions tutor for the department in which you want to study. If you already have some GCSE, GCE 'O' level and GCE 'A' level subject passes, you may be ready to enter without further preparation, or you may be advised to take one or two additional subjects in support of your application. If you have been away from study for a long time, you will probably be advised to ease your way into the right level of concentration again through a suitable pre-degree preparatory course. These courses are usually called 'access courses' and are run locally throughout the country by further education colleges and organisations such as the Open College,which operates the same kind of open admissions policy as the Open University. They are also provided by the extra-mural studies departments of the universities, polytechnics and higher education colleges who are offering the degree courses that students want access to, thus giving the student a first step on the ladder.

At the APL stage of *gathering evidence* that we considered in Unit 3 (Figure 3.4), whoever is responsible for dealing with your mature student application for an access place will talk to you personally, by telephone and face-to-face, and will almost certainly ask you to do a short piece of written work, perhaps a few hundred words, in order to assess your existing writing skills. Do not be afraid to commit yourself to expressing your ideas in writing as well as through speaking. Almost all of your degree-level course work will need to be done through the written medium, and it is vital that you get the necessary preparation to enable you to cope.

It is very important at this early stage not only to emphasise what strengths you have, but to acknowledge honestly to yourself as a prospective undergraduate student what you feel your areas of weakness are. People who have had almost entirely practical jobs may lack experience and confidence in written work. Many people feel shaky about basic maths and try to avoid dealing with anything numerical. This is unwise and unnecessary, as most subjects now require students to be able to take a numerical and statistical approach to the study material, and there are many basic courses for adults which can help. If you need to acquire mathematical or computer skills, do it now. You will have more time and opportunity during your access year than at any time later during your course.

As a result of interviewing you and making an appraisal of any tests or written exercises that you have been asked to do, your access counsellor will be able to form an opinion about how ready you are to undertake your pre-undergraduate year of access study. This is the *assessment* stage of APL (Figure 3.4) and, as there is no formal *accreditation* needed here, the counsellor will give you immediate *post-assessment guidance* about whether or not they think eventual degree-level study is a suitable option for you. If they think it is not, they will explain why and help you to consider what other alternatives are available to you. They may even invite you to attend an access course anyway, should you wish, for your own educational and personal development. This will leave open to you the possibility that your situation can be reviewed later, in the light of changes, improvements and developments in your work.

Your access counsellor will also advise you when it is appropriate for you to begin your access studies. These usually follow the higher education academic year from October through to June and lead towards entry into a degree course in the next academic year. How and when you need to make your degree course application, and how full- and part-time degree courses are organised, will be dealt with in Unit 5. The access year course itself will take you through the process of acquiring the personal, organisational and study skills you need to undertake advanced study. What these skills are we shall look at in Units 9 to 15, and I should like to call them *student competences*, in line with the NCVQ thinking we saw in Unit 3. At the end of this unit you will be asked to do some work on thinking about your own student competences and about which areas you need to work on to establish the kind of student profile you will need for success.

A typical access year will require a study commitment of four or five hours per week class attendance spread over two 10-week terms, plus an extra five or six weeks during the summer term. This gives a total of somewhere between 100 and 130 part-time student hours during the year. The student is expected to contribute at least this amount again in home study, so that you need to be prepared for at least five hours home study per week, arranged as a daily or twice-weekly commitment as you wish. The combined total of class attendance and home study hours will be somewhere between 200 and 260 hours over the course of the year. For distance-learning students this will need to be done by home study only. The Open University, which allows open and immediate access to anyone wishing to study for a degree, regardless of previous experience, have their own preparatory study skills package to help students get to the level the Open University requires for degree course entry.

A typical access year could cost around £85, at 1992 prices, with a reduction to around £75 for a distance-learning arrangement. To this you would need to add the cost of recommended books, writing materials and travelling, if appropriate. Many institutions offer a reduced fee to unemployed people, and to anyone solely dependent on benefits or retirement pensions as income.

## What can I do to get funding?

All the numerical information about costs and funding given here is approximate and based on current figures. Costs, needless to say, increase every year along with inflation. Funding, on the other hand, doesn't, and can stay static for years at a time, until the government or the administrators of the funding make a change; and it isn't always an increase. The information given here will be out of date by the time this book goes to press, and further out of date by the time you read it. The figures can change at any time with a change in government policy or a change in government, so they are meant to draw attention to what you need to think about, and it is left to you to find out current figures at the time of reading from the sources of information indicated here and the addresses given at the end of the book.

The Open University gives a very clear breakdown of study costs and arrangements in their guide to the BA Degree Programme. The basic BA degree requires the student to gain six study credits, usually over five or six years. The first year of OU study at 1992 prices could cost around £450, including tuition, study materials, books, travel and accommodation for a summer school, and incidental expenses such as postage, telephone contact with tutors and travel to tutorials. For students living outside the UK, the estimated cost would be nearer £750. Tuition fees alone account for about £250 of this on a single credit course. So you are looking at a commitment of something like £3,000 over the next few years, allowing for annual fee increases. Students can pay by monthly instalments, so you would need to have available about £40 per month to cover fees and other expenses.

A typical part-time degree course taken extra-murally is that offered by Manchester University, which requires the student to complete 10 modules for the basic BA Degree, at a cost of £150 per module. This means a total cost of £1,500, indexed upwards annually with inflation, over the usual five or six years for the course. Payment can be made in two instalments annually and covers tuition fees only. The course is conducted on a class-contact basis, with one evening attendance per week per module, supported by private study.

The Local Education Authority (LEA) of your district of residence is responsible for administering student grants for approved study courses. Some of them are able to give financial help for parts of an Open University or part-time degree course; others do not, as part-time study is a discretionary area of their responsibilities. Some employers will give financial assistance for part-time degree study; the important thing for the prospective student to do is to ask, and to make out a good case for the support they want.

If you are in the fortunate position of being able to withdraw from work for the three to four years that a full-time degree course will take, and if you are a British national normally resident in UK, you will be legally entitled to a mandatory student grant, provided that you have not had one before and that your existing income does not exceed a certain level. A previous grant for part of a degree course will alter your entitlement to the full amount, as will failing to meet the precise requirements for normal residence. So it's a matter of making a grant application, knowing your rights, being prepared to make out a good case on your own behalf, but accepting that, ultimately, individual LEAs have discretionary power rather than mandatory responsibility in certain borderline areas of interpreting grant regulations, and that all you can do if they finally say 'No' is to change your district of residence; a rather drastic step. How and when to apply for a grant we will look at in Unit 5.

The grant figures quoted here are an approximate guide and are based on 1991–2 levels. Unfortunately, while fees, maintenance expenses and other course costs keep going up, grants don't. So don't do any index-linking on your calculations here, or you could find yourself way out in balancing your budget. As a mature student who is not dependent on parental support, you would probably receive about £2,250 per year maintenance grant, in addition to tuition fees which are paid directly to your study institution. There is an increase to about £2,850 if you study in London, and there can be extra allowances if you are disabled, or if you have dependants to support. On the other hand, if your spouse earns more than £10,000 per year, he or she can be asked to make a graded contribution to your maintenance. This starts at £10 minimum, and finishes at £5,800 maximum if your spouse earns more than £39,000 per year. This could in fact wipe out your entire entitlement to a grant, even given the various additional allowances you may be eligible for.

One source of additional student income that is not dependent on the financial situation of parents or spouse, or on your own existing income or financial prospects, is the student loan. Student loans are administered by the government-run Student Loans Company whose address is given at the end of this book. The maximum loan for a mature student is £715 per year at 1992–3 rates, and it needs to be re-applied for annually. It has to be repaid, with interest index-linked to inflation, by monthly instalments from April of the year following the end of your course. So it is not a commitment to be undertaken lightly and you do need to be able to get back into work fairly promptly at the end of your course; but it is not difficult to get in the first place, unless you are aged 50 or over. The government has also made available to higher education institutions additional money known as 'access funds', to allow them to give some discretionary help to students facing prohibitive financial difficulties. This help is only available by special application to your educational institution, but it does not have to be repaid and there is no age limit.

The Open University is the main provider of distance-learning degree-level study in the UK and it has its own funds for assisting low-income students who cannot get help from LEAs or employers. The OU student fees section should be approached by anyone who has been accepted on an OU course but who doubts their ability to pay. The OU also has additional resources from various funds, trusts and bursaries, which are administered by the OU on a discretionary basis. For non-OU students, public libraries throughout the country carry copies of *The Grants Register* for the current year, and other directories of educational trusts, charities and foundations which might be of help to individual students wanting particular courses. Details of some of these are given at the end of this book. Career development loans are offered for one year only by three banks: Barclays, the Clydesdale and the Co-operative, on behalf of the Department of Employment. The amount can be up to £5,000, depending on the course costs, and the loans are available for specifically vocationally-oriented courses. How and when to apply for a student loan will be looked at in Unit 5.

If you are resident in Scotland, or would like to go to a Scottish university, you need to be aware of some differences in the system that could affect your advance planning. The Scottish Certificate of Education (SCE) is taken at the age of 15 or 16 by young people in school or college, who usually obtain up to seven 'S' grades which are roughly comparable with GCSE or the former GCE 'O' level in the rest of UK. They take a further five subjects at higher 'H' level one year later and are ready to enter higher education at age 17, the Scottish degree course being of four years duration rather than three, and leading to the award of a first degree at Master's rather than Bachelor's level. *The Scottish University Entrance Guide* can give more information about individual universities and about features of organisation that are a little different, but the method of application through the University Central Council for Admissions (UCCA) is the same, and the method of grant and loan application is the same as for the rest of the UK.

## EXERCISES ON STUDENT COMPETENCES

**Figure 4.1 shows the 10 most important competences that you will need to have as a mature returner to work and study.**

***Units of competence 1 to 5*** **are often called** ***'personal effectiveness traits'*** **and they are equally important in work, study and private life. They can be broken down into** ***elements of competence*****, and when you do this you will find that many of the work and personal management skills that you explored in Unit 3 have a place in the scheme. These are your existing** ***transferable skills*****.**

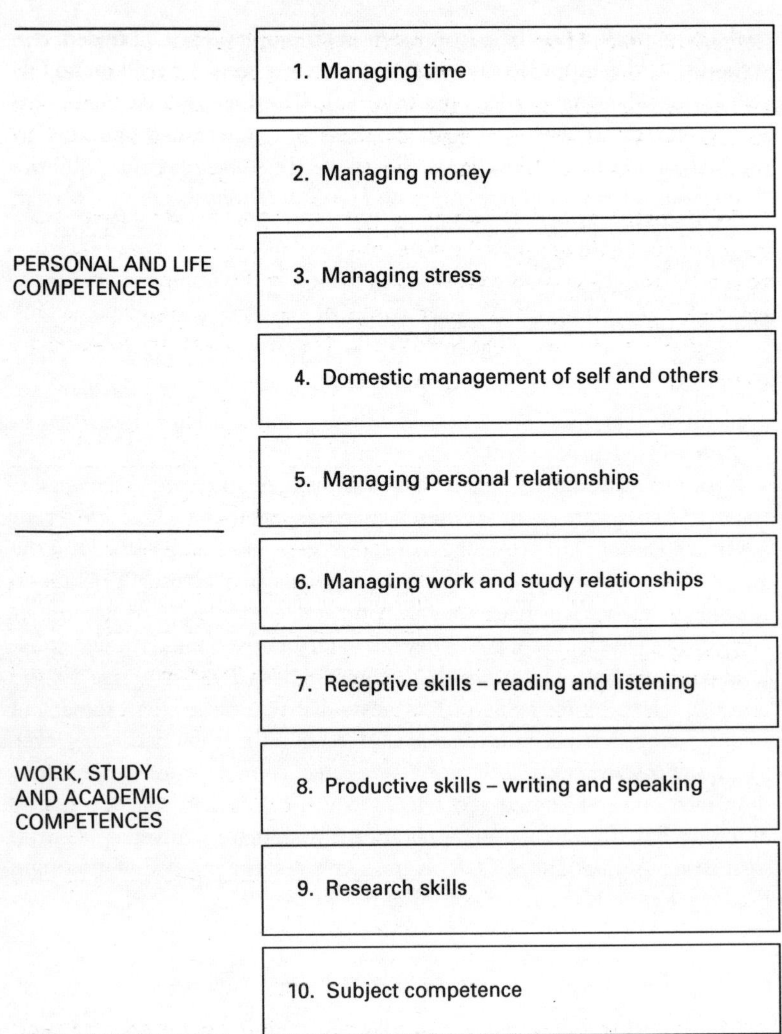

PERSONAL AND LIFE COMPETENCES
1. Managing time
2. Managing money
3. Managing stress
4. Domestic management of self and others
5. Managing personal relationships
WORK, STUDY AND ACADEMIC COMPETENCES
6. Managing work and study relationships
7. Receptive skills – reading and listening
8. Productive skills – writing and speaking
9. Research skills
10. Subject competence


Figure 4.1 *Units of student competence*

***Units of competence 6 to 10*** **are *work-related competences*, when you regard being a student as a full-time job equivalent. They too can be broken down into *elements of competence*, but the content and emphasis will vary more from subject to subject (or job to job) and**

not all of your Unit 3 *transferable skills* may find a place in the scheme. There will also be other skills that you need to develop to complete this skills profile, and later units in this book will help you to analyse what the required *elements of competence* are and to build them up into the *units of competence* of Figure 4.1.

*Units of competence 6 to 10* will require much additional help from your tutors to develop and refine, particularly your subject competence 10 and your research skills 9, which will be strongly subject-related. Everything else in your range of student competences this book will be able to help you with. We will start by looking at *student competence 2:* managing money.

| | ELEMENTS OF COMPETENCE | |
|---|---|---|
| **Unit of competence 2:** Managing money | Balancing annual income against outgoings | Current solvency |
| | Managing cash flow | |
| | Finding course expenses | |
| | Making investments | Long-term solvency |
| | Acquiring capital | |

Figure 4.2 *Managing money*

The first three *elements of competence* in Figure 4.2 mean that you must have enough money for weekly, monthly and annual bills and expenditure, as well as routine daily expenses, and this is what we shall concentrate on here. These lead to the *performance criteria* which show that you actually have the competence to manage your money routinely, and hopefully to keep something in reserve for emergencies and for the long-term future. Meeting the *performance criteria* is when you have actually done what the *element of competence* claims you are able to do.

**Your task over the next few months, preferably over a full year, is to keep detailed accounts of your household and personal expenditure, and to compare it with your annual income from all sources, including any regular augmentation from benefits or investment income. From the information given in this unit, estimate your annual course expenses and see how you can arrange to have enough money to become a student. Analyse your household and personal expenditure under the following suggested headings, adding your own if these are insufficient:**

***ESSENTIALS:***

***Housing costs***
**Mortgage/rent**
**Insurance**
**Poll Tax**
**Loan repayments**
**Building maintenance**
**(Committed savings)**
**(Long-term investments)**

***Household running expenses***
**Furnishing and soft furnishing**
**Internal maintenance and decoration**
**Equipment purchase & maintenance, eg, cookers, fridges, freezers, washers.**
**Gas, electricity**
**Telephone rental and bills**
**Cleaning materials and services**
**Gardening costs**

***Food and health***
**Meals at home**
**Meals at work**
**Doctors' prescriptions**
**Dental and opticians' charges**
**Private health insurance**
**Life insurance**
**Routine medicines and toiletries, eg, aspirins, toothpaste, soap, etc.**

***Clothing***
**For self and family**
**Shoes and shoe repairs**
**Cleaning and laundry**
**Hairdressing**

***BASICS:***

***Travel expenses***
**Car-purchase, road tax, petrol, insurance,**

***Child care***
**Services of nanny**
**Nursery place/s**

maintenance and repair (include annual depreciation)
Bus and train fares
Taxis
Other work-related expenses not tax deductible
Child-minder services

*EXTRAS*:

*Holidays*
Travel
Accommodation
Activities
Weekends away
Days out

*Interests and hobbies*
Sport and recreation
Entertainments

*Home comforts*
TV and radio
Stereo and video
Newspapers
Magazines
Alcohol
Cigarettes

*Social and personal*
Christmas
Birthdays
Parties, presents
Meals out
Personal treats

Assign your own priorities to whether things are essential, basic or extra. Look towards the bottom of the list to see where temporary economies can be made. If you are living beyond your income look at the top of the list to see where changes can be made in the interests of permanent economies.

# II
# MOVING IN

## UNIT 5. Setting Objectives

Here and in Unit 6 we consider how someone who wants to take a degree, whether full-time or part-time, needs to plan their moves in line with the timescale set by the higher education institutions or the Open University. Before you consider access courses or grant applications you need to know at what point in time you aim to enter the system at degree level. You should also have a clear plan about how long you would like to remain in the system before you graduate, other things being equal. People taking the part-time external degree or Open University route may need a strong element of flexibility here, depending on their personal circumstances. What is not flexible is the beginning and end of the academic year and the dates of final examinations. There are certain points at which, however flexible your study arrangements, you have to fit into the system, or wait another year.

### When should I apply for a higher education place?

The academic year for universities, polytechnics and higher education colleges runs from the beginning of October through to the end of the following June, ending usually in sessional examinations, with final examinations in May or June of the final year of the course. These institutions start to think about their degree level admissions early on in the year of the October entry. Young people in schools and further education colleges, using the traditional GCE 'A' level entry route, have to have their course applications with supporting references finalised and submitted by December of the previous year, almost a year in advance. They can expect to be interviewed sometime between February and April prior to the October entry, and will, if they are lucky, have some provisional offers of places made to them before they sit final GCE 'A' level examinations in June.

If you are entering a full-time higher education degree course using the traditional GCE 'A' level route, you need to know what courses you would be interested in being offered a place on, and what institutions offer these courses, a year in advance. If you are working towards taking 'A' levels, either full-time as a further-education student, or by flexi-study or distance-learning arrangements with a college, the college is responsible for dealing with your application for a higher education place by submitting your application with a supporting reference before the closing date for applications in December. The application goes to the University Central Council for Admissions (UCCA) or the Polytechnic Central Admissions System (PCAS), and your application will then be processed along with the many thousands of others from the younger generation of students, with whom you will be competing for what may be a scarcity of places in very popular subjects.

If you are a student who is not part of the further education system, perhaps because you already have enough GCE 'O' or GCSE and 'A' level passes to meet higher education entry requirements from your earlier education, you will need to approach the admissions bodies yourself and ask for their advice about how to proceed. Their addresses are given at the end of this book. What the admissions bodies can do, that is difficult to do for yourself, is to process your application in such a way that you make several choices in order of preference, and should you fail to meet the examination pass grades required by your first choice institution, the bodies will pass your application down the line until they find one who will offer you a place. There are also clearance arrangements for unplaced students to be matched up with unoccupied places once public examination results are available in mid-August. If you want a full-time higher education place, UCCA and PCAS are the ways to get choice initially, and a fall-back position if things don't work out exactly as you hope; this is how most UK students get their full-time higher education places.

The initial work of deciding which full-time higher education course you want, and which institutions offer it in which parts of the country, is up to you. Some of the excellent published guidebooks for prospective university entrants are listed at the end of this book, but the work of writing round to universities, polytechnics and higher education colleges for their undergraduate prospectuses is yours. The admissions bodies can only help you when you know what you want. If you already do know what you want, and where you would like to go to get it, it is worth writing to the student admissions officer in the registrar's department of the institution concerned, to see if you can make a direct application. If you have the option of studying in a different part of the country, or even in another country for part of your course, it is worth thinking about how to get the best for yourself from a unique life opportunity.

You will also, I hope, be beginning to see the need for long-term life planning. You need to start at least a year in advance, planning and finding a place on the course you want. Add to this three or four years of study, and you can see the need for thinking five years ahead. We shall work on this in Unit 8.

Most prospective mature students will be thinking of a part-time external degree course at their nearest university or an Open University degree course, probably taking five or six years to complete. If you are taking a one-year access course at your nearest university or polytechnic, or at a local further education college which has special links with a particular university or polytechnic, you will be in a more favourable position to get a place on a degree or diploma course at the university or polytechnic concerned. You will spend your access year acquiring the organisational and study skills needed to undertake an advanced study course, rather than struggling to get the appropriate 'A' level grades and subjects. You will be moving towards higher education entry by a special arrangement for mature students and, while short-cutting the 'A' level route has its advantages, there are some snags, such as having a more limited choice of degree course subjects.

The Open University academic year runs from February to October and within these nine months your study commitment will need to be well-organised and undertaken regularly, in order to cope with continuous assessment and, usually, final examinations in October. Offers of places are made between March and September of the previous year, so that your choice of foundation course and tentative plans for gaining future credits need to be made up to a year in advance of the February entry date. The Open University has links with the National Extension College, which offers a wide range of distance-learning courses that lead into the OU degree level programme. Contact addresses are given at the end of this book. You will see the need for long-term planning when you think of the time-scale for access, entry, higher education and then a degree course spread over five or six years. You will need to think at least seven years ahead in your life, and even as much as 10 years if you want to allow your degree course to take longer.

## When do I apply for a grant or a loan?

If you are entering a full-time higher education degree or diploma course, you should apply for a grant almost as soon as you make your higher education application, though not earlier than January for a course starting in the following October. You should not wait until you receive clear acceptance on the course you want, as a late grant application may mean delayed payment of money that you urgently need. You only need to make a single grant application for the whole of your full-time course, but you need to remember that annual renewal of your grant does depend on satisfactory progress in your course, and that your institution may be asked to report on this by your grant-awarding body. This is part of the contract that you make with both of them, and we shall look at what underlies making these contracts in Unit 6.

A grant award is made for a specific course at a specified institution by the local education authority (LEA) of your district of residence. Should you for any reason need or decide to change course, institution or district of residence, the grant application procedure will have to be repeated with your new LEA.

Your grant application should be made to the LEA of your district of residence, and they will ask you to complete three forms at different stages:

1. *An application form*, to establish whether or not you are entitled to a grant.
2. *A grant-assessment form*, which will enable your LEA to decide how much you should receive.

You will need to get your spouse's cooperation, if you are married, in completing this second form, just as younger applicants have to get their parents' cooperation. If they do not, for whatever reason, give information about their income and other details as requested, you will receive no maintenance grant to help with your living costs. You may not need this financial help if you intend to continue living at home, but if you are giving up a job to become a student, and if you have been making a significant contribution to your household income, you should take advantage of any grant entitlement you have. You can expect to be asked to complete this form each year to check that the amount for which you are eligible has remained the same.

3. *A college-acceptance form*, which you should send to your higher education institution as soon as it has made you an unconditional offer of a place and you know you want to accept.

If your acceptance depends on examination results, you should send this form as soon as they are known. The institution will complete the form, confirming your acceptance on your course, and return it to your LEA, who will now make their final decision about your eligibility for a grant and the amount to be offered. Your LEA will normally send you an award letter confirming their offer. They will pay your tuition fees directly to the institution, and will normally send your grant cheque to the college office for you to collect at the start of each term. The office will often put up a notice, with the names of students whose grant cheques are available to be collected, at the beginning of each term.

You cannot apply for a student loan until you have actually started your course. The government-administered Students Loans Company provides your higher education institution with the information and application forms you need in order to apply for a student loan, and your institution has to certify your eligibility. You can normally apply for a loan at any time during the academic year, but the Student Loans Company will not negotiate loans after 31 July in the year for which you want to receive the loan. If you wish to repeat your loan application in subsequent years you will need to go through the same procedures each year. It is important to check through in detail the conditions for repaying student loans, and satisfy yourself that you can meet them, before taking on what initially looks to be a tempting offer.

If you are approaching any of the independent grant-awarding bodies, such as those included in the Grants Register or the Educational Grants Directory, you will again be competing for limited funds and an early application is advisable. It is also important to realise the value of making a strong case in support of your application, and some of the ideas put forward in the last four units of this book might be of help to you in doing this.

If you are a person on very low income, not eligible for a loan or grant for whatever reasons, you may be able to obtain financial help from the government-allocated access funds available for distribution by your educational institution. The best approach is to obtain an offer of a place on the course you want, and then approach the institution with evidence of your financial situation. The Open University especially recommend this, and will help from their own sources of funding anyone who would otherwise be unable to take the course they want.

If you take out a student loan it is important to realise how this alters the time-scale of your advance planning. Your repayments will commence in the April following the end of your course and will be made by direct debit from your bank or building society account in monthly instalments over five years. The unpaid amount outstanding will be annually index-linked to inflation, so that the value of the sum you repay will be the same, in real terms, as the value of the sum borrowed five years earlier. In a period of high inflation this could be a considerable erosion of your earnings during the first few years of your career, should you have even a moderately paid job. To the time of four to five years, estimated for one year of access study followed by three to four years for a full-time degree course, you can add five years more for getting student loan repayments off your back. So you need to do your financial sums and life-planning rather carefully.

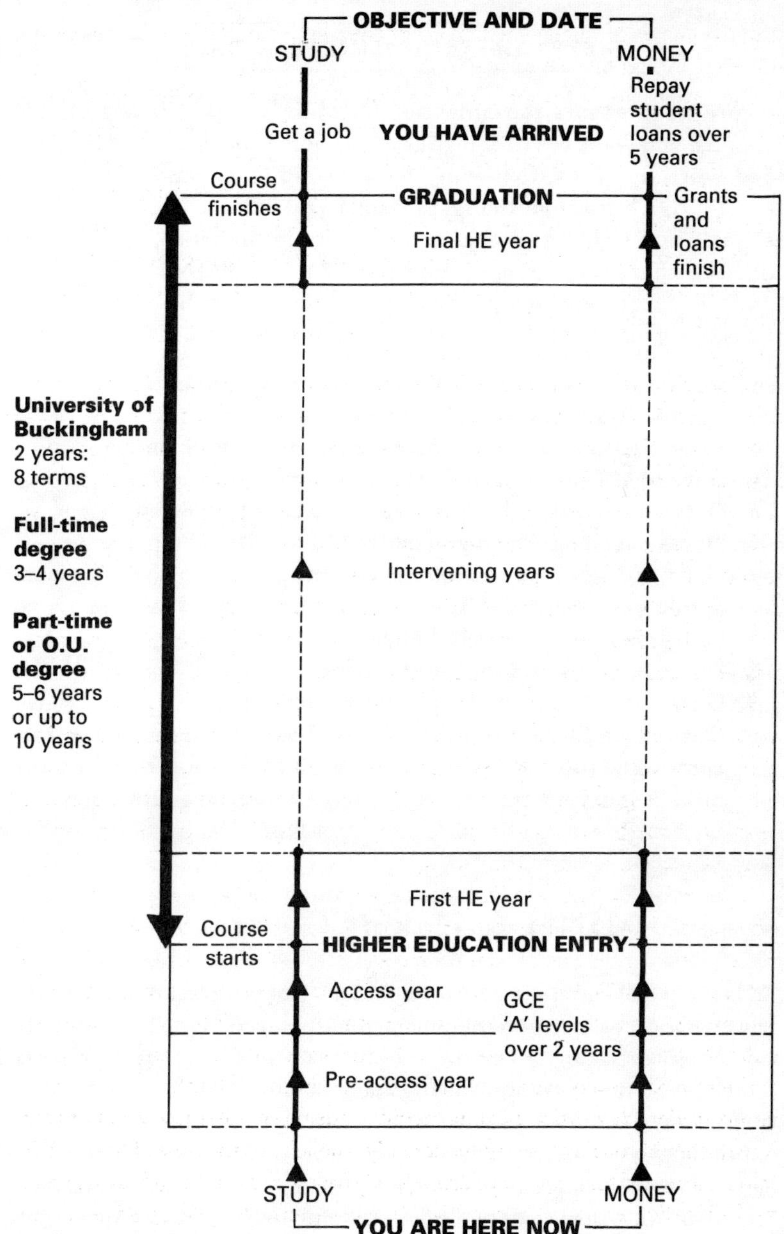


Figure 5 *Planning ahead – studying and money*

### EXERCISES ON ADVANCE PLANNING

**Figure 5 represents the timescale on which you will have to think ahead if you want to enter higher education. Start from the bottom and work upwards, following the arrowed lines marked STUDY and MONEY through the system until you emerge at the top. Use the left and right hand columns to write in (in pencil, in case you need to change your mind) your STUDY and MONEY objectives and the dates by which you need to achieve them. Be as precise as possible, giving month and year where you need to:**

1. **Decide what you would like to study and where.**
2. **Calculate the cost of your course expenses.**
3. **Date of entry to access course or GCE 'A' level course.**
4. **Date of UCCA application form submission.**
5. **Dates between which you expect to be interviewed.**
6. **Dates between which you expect to be offered a place.**
7. **Date of higher education entry, remembering that the academic year normally starts in October, but that the Open University year starts in February.**
8. **Dates of grant and loan applications.**
9. **Dates when grant and loan instalments are due.**
10. **Date of graduation and date by which loan repayments must be completed (don't be afraid to go beyond the year 2000 into the next century if your course is going to be a long one).**

## UNIT 6. Making Contracts

When you fill in an application form for a student place on a course and sign your name declaring your commitment, you are embarking on an undertaking as serious as taking a job and signing your agreement to your future employer's terms of contract and conditions of service. I'd like to suggest here that you view becoming a student as seriously as you view being or becoming a paid employee. In terms of the time, effort, organisation and energy you will invest in a demanding course of study, there isn't that much difference. If you are a part-time, flexi-study or distance-learning student, the demands on you will be even greater. If someone is absent from work due to sickness, or for some unavoidable reason, their colleagues usually manage without them.

Whatever you miss from a study course you have to make up in your own time.

## What am I agreeing to with my college or university?

Colleges, polytechnics and universities have their own sets of regulations that students are expected to comply with, and indeed when you sign your application form you are agreeing to do so. It's much the same as agreeing to what an employer expects of you in a job, although as a student you will largely be expected to discipline yourself, and the ultimate sanction will not be dismissal but failure to get the qualification you want. Regulations for students are usually stated in very general ways as regards study, but they do require punctuality and regularity in attendance at classes and prompt submission of course assignments. On the discipline side, prompt payment of fees is appreciated, though if you are a grant-aided student that may be out of your control; and you will be expected to deal with your own examination entries.

What you are really agreeing to when you register as a student is the hidden agenda, the acceptance on your part that you will allow yourself to be taught certain things to a certain level, and guided along certain lines of educational development, by your tutors on behalf of the institution. The undertaking on their part is that they will do this for you. It is a matter of trust that you allow this, as you cannot know yourself what you need to know and must allow more experienced people to judge for you. You must let them set the objectives for you and help you to attain them. What you will learn during this process is how to achieve greater independence as a learner and ultimately how to teach yourself. The final qualification you leave with is in many ways just another starting point, but what you will have learned as part of the educational experience is how to move yourself on, not just now but always.

There is also an implicit agreement that you value the professional services of the people who deal with you in your college or university and that you try to make it as easy as possible for them to do their best for you. You are one among thousands, or tens of thousands, for the institution, and one among hundreds for the people who deal with you on a day-to-day basis. The more you show them the courtesy of realising this, the greater will be the reliability and trust developed between you. Not only tutors, lecturers and research supervisors are important; administrative and secretarial staff, librarians and audio-visual and laboratory technician staff all have an important part to play in getting you through the system. In your job of work as a student these are your fellow employees, just as your fellow students are your colleagues, and you would expect to try to get on with them and gain the cooperation and support which can make so much difference to your own progress.

## What am I agreeing to with whoever is funding my study?

If you are paying for yourself, wholly and entirely, you have no responsibility to be financially accountable to anyone else. You still have the more legal kind of responsibility to keep your contract as a student with your educational institution, and you have a moral responsibility to make the best use of your student place that you possibly can. Tutors' time and the institution's resources are valuable, and your place could be being occupied by someone else who might make better use of the opportunity.

However, most students are in no such lucky position as to be able to finance themselves, and they will be in receipt of grant-aid from their LEA, scholarships or awards from government or other bodies and possible additional student loans to be repaid later. All of these sources of finance make funding available for the specific purpose of following a study course leading to a stated outcome, and your educational institution may be required to offer evidence at regular intervals that this is what you are doing. Thus it is important to maintain attendance and work schedules at the expected level of commitment, as you could otherwise find yourself having your grant renewal queried and needing to justify that you are making proper use of a supported student place. You are financially accountable to whoever your sponsoring body is, as you are receiving help from public funds, and when you are a tax-payer yourself you are quick enough to resent any waste of public money. If you are in receipt of a private grant, the trustees of the award system will want to know that the monies are being used effectively. If you have a loan, creditors will want to think that you are a responsible borrower who can be relied on to pay back.

## What am I agreeing to with my partner or family, now and later?

You should, if you possibly can, get the support and agreement of your partner and family voluntarily, before you move towards insisting that returning to work or study is what you intend to do and that they must adjust to the changes. The stages of arguments, explanations, justifications and reasonable requests should be worked through patiently and thoroughly before you put your foot down and say that this is what is going to happen. You need at this point to tell them what you are going to do, not why.

Re-arrange domestic schedules where possible to suit yourself as well as others. Tell everyone what you expect them to do, when, and in full detail, and have a daily, weekly and monthly schedule or calendar in a prominent place in the house where everyone can refer to it easily. Much of what goes on in domestic life runs through on a well-understood routine and what you are asking for is just a different routine. One routine is not much different from another once people get used to it, and your family will gain in flexibility and adaptability by learning to accommodate change in life. Let it be clear to everyone that if they fail to do whatever is their share in the daily household routine, you will not pick up the tab for them. What they fail to complete will remain undone until they deal with it and if it's something important that they want, they will go without it. You yourself, as an adult, must take on the sharing and planning of household finance and major commitments with your partner, if you have one. Children can be told what to do, but they should not be expected to think things through for you or make decisions beyond their competence.

## What am I agreeing with myself, for now and later?

You need to accept and agree with yourself that, whatever else you are doing by going back to work or study, you are altering your self-image permanently. Once you make this move you will never ever see yourself in the same light again. You will become, not necessarily a different person, but a much more experienced and developed person. You will know this yourself unmistakeably and the people in closest touch with your ideas and feelings will know it. There will be some people who will not realise that something profoundly important has happened in your life and that you have changed because of it and, regrettably, some of these may be, if not exactly your nearest and dearest, at least people whom you would have preferred to have with you. What to do about this possibility is something we shall think about in the closing units of this book.

If you are returning to study you are investing a considerable amount of time, energy and money in your own life and future. Other people will benefit from this, if only because you become happier and more self-fulfilled as a person and your way of dealing with life and relationships becomes much better. In a sense it is irrelevant who else benefits incidentally; you have a right to do this for yourself and are not just here as an enabler for others. As you embark on your course of study leading to a professional or practical qualification, or return to work to follow a career path or take on new job responsibilities, what is ahead of you is a massive life change with all the stresses that involves, and at the end of it you will no longer want to go back to the old ways of living and being. You yourself will have changed so much that you will no longer fit.

## EXERCISES ON MANAGING WORK/STUDY RELATIONSHIPS

| Unit of competence 6 | PERFORMANCE CRITERIA |
|---|---|
| **Unit of competence 6:** Managing work/study relationships | Can get on with fellow students |
| | Can get on with tutors and lecturers |
| | Can get on with research supervisor |
| | Can get on with AV and technician staff |
| | Can get on with admin. staff |
| | Can get on with secretarial staff |
| | |
| | |

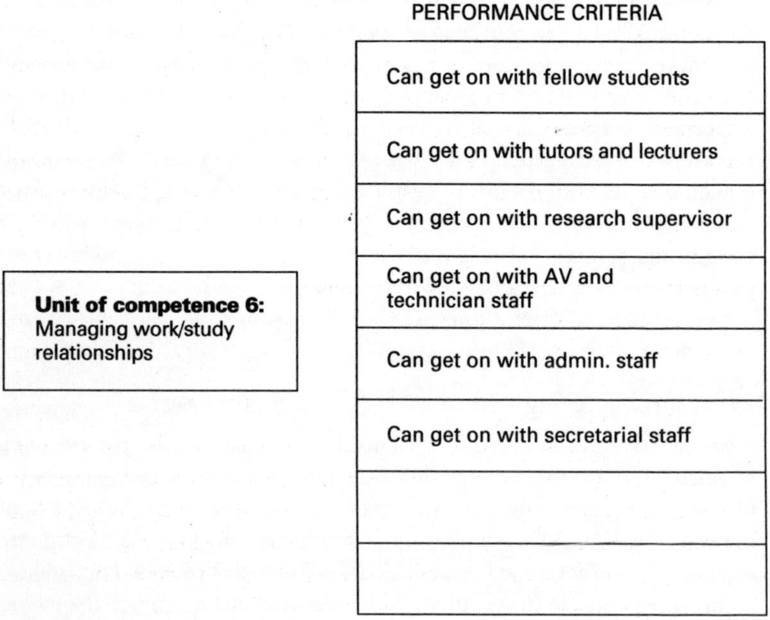

Figure 6 *Managing work/study relationships*

**Taking *unit of competence 6* from Figure 4.1 in Unit 4, *elements of competence* have been merged with *performance criteria* in Figure 6. These are all the people with whom you should be on good working or professional terms. You may add others of your own, such as library staff and key members of the caretaking and maintenance staff and senior management. Focus on any relationships that are poor or ineffective and see if you can find ways of improving them using key skills of negotiation, cooperation, appreciation and assertion. Assertion is better used sparingly and with persuasion as many people who are either passive or over-assertive themselves do not understand it and fail to appreciate it.**

# UNIT 7. Seeking Support

An idea I want to advance here is that two things we all need to deal with in our personal lives are *change* and *continuity*. Some things change, in ways that make us no longer want to retain them as part of our lives, and we need to be willing and know how to let them go. Other things change, but they are important enough to us to make us want to adapt to the change, so that we can keep them in our lives. I want to take the point of view that our family relationships need flexibility as well as continuity, but that there are other relationships that we can set up and develop for ourselves, outside the circle of family and existing friends, and that these can be relationships of our own choice at specific times and for specific reasons.

Getting together a group of people who are interested in what you are doing as a mature student and in your progress is one of the most important personal things you can do, both before you start your study course and as you go on. This will be your personal support network, as you go through the processes and crises of being a returner to study, and later move on into work or whatever your subsequent lifestyle is going to be. Your relationships with people in your personal support network will need to be set up along the lines you want, maintained all along so that they are there when you need them, and made worthwhile for the other people as well as yourself; support between adult people should always be a two-way process. We shall look later at what your specific support needs are, and at who could possibly meet them.

## What kind of support do I need?

It will be helpful here to look at the results of American research by Gail Sheehy, D.J.Levinson and others on the stages and tasks of adult life, as summarised in Figure 7.1.

The researchers emphasise that the transition age from one stage to the next is approximate, and that the transition process is not instantaneous. People carry forward with them through life any incomplete tasks or unresolved problems, and ultimately these have to be dealt with if the person is to function as a mature adult of whatever age. The research also emphasises that becoming a mature adult is a social as well as a personal process, and that the transition stages would be expected to be at different points for different people, at different points for men and women, and at different points for people living at different times in history, or in different societies or cultures now. We will reassess these research findings later, in view of the current situation of high unemployment and poor job prospects in the UK.

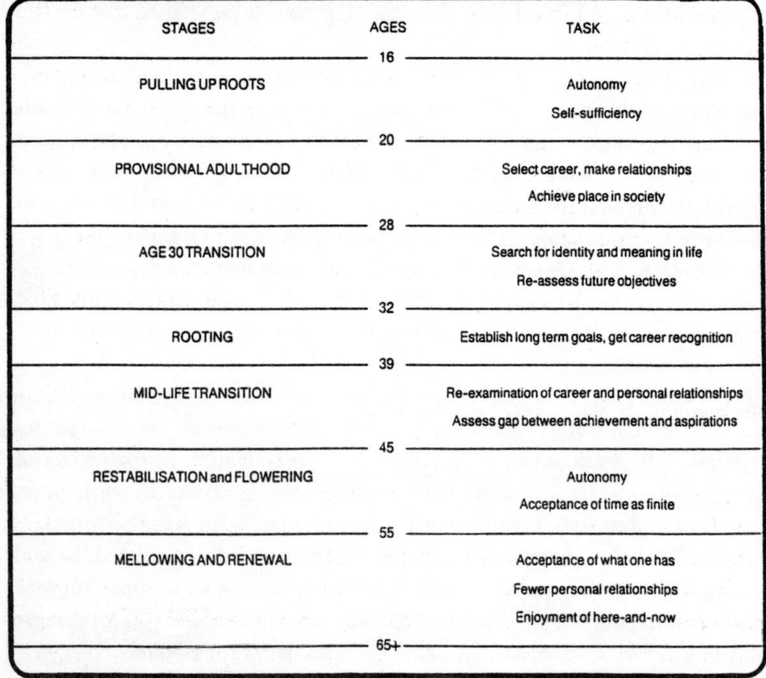

| STAGES | AGES | TASK |
|---|---|---|
| | 16 | |
| PULLING UP ROOTS | | Autonomy<br>Self-sufficiency |
| | 20 | |
| PROVISIONAL ADULTHOOD | | Select career, make relationships<br>Achieve place in society |
| | 28 | |
| AGE 30 TRANSITION | | Search for identity and meaning in life<br>Re-assess future objectives |
| | 32 | |
| ROOTING | | Establish long term goals, get career recognition |
| | 39 | |
| MID-LIFE TRANSITION | | Re-examination of career and personal relationships<br>Assess gap between achievement and aspirations |
| | 45 | |
| RESTABILISATION and FLOWERING | | Autonomy<br>Acceptance of time as finite |
| | 55 | |
| MELLOWING AND RENEWAL | | Acceptance of what one has<br>Fewer personal relationships<br>Enjoyment of here-and-now |
| | 65+ | |

Figure 7.1 *Stages and tasks of adulthood*

The key to personal life development through the stages of Figure 7.1 is to negotiate the transitions successfully, and to do that the person undergoing the transition needs to be aware of it. There are three stages to a life transition: separation from the previous stage, an intermediate state of flux, and settling into the new stage. For the younger person starting their first job, getting a new job, or getting married, the first and last stages are usually clearly marked by physically moving house or place of work. For the older person retiring from work perhaps earlier than they want to, or the person of any age who loses their job through redundancy and has to face unemployment, or the person coming back to study after leaving work or bringing up a family at home, it is the middle stage of going through a state of flux that can be overwhelmingly confusing and stressful.

We noted that the ages at which the life transitions of Figure 7.1 occur will vary with the social conditions and pressures of the time we live in. The difficulty younger people now experience in finding a permanent job, or indeed any kind of job, can postpone provisional adulthood and disturb the time-scale of all the stages that follow. People who face loss of a job at any age will have difficulty setting longer term life and career goals, and those who face repeated redundancy will have problems getting any career recognition from anybody. Many people now retire early, not necessarily willingly, and have neither the money nor the inclination to flower and mellow into a fruitful old age. People living alone, with or without children, but with no adult support on a day-to-day basis, may not follow the Figure 7.1 time-scale in the same way at all, and will certainly find the transitions more stressful because of having to negotiate them alone. These are society's invisible people, there are many of them, and they deserve a book of their own.

## Where shall I get moral support?

The set of concentric circles in Figure 7.2 is a simple but convenient way of representing any one of us in our life situation, surrounded by family, friends, neighbours, colleagues, people in the street and society in general. The letters from A to F mark the degree of closeness we feel to particular individuals and the importance to us of what we share with them. You, the person, with your most personal private thoughts and feelings, are alone in the middle at A, at least to start with. Level F marks the area in which your contacts with your fellow-members of society and the human race are at their least personal. This is the level of contact and communication at which you encounter cashiers in the supermarket, ticket clerks at the train station booking office, and strangers who say good-morning in the street. Level F is not unimportant; far from it; but it is not close and the contacts made are usually transient.

Anyone with whom you feel you can share your most private and personal thoughts and feelings, in an atmosphere of confidentiality and acceptance, gets admitted to level A. This level of communication and relatedness I am going to call 'intimacy', meaning personal intimacy as distinct from sexual intimacy. It is to be hoped that spouses, partners, family and some friends are with us at level A; but it is asking a lot of just one person, however close. Some would say that it is asking too much, and that we need at least a few people with whom to share this intimate level of communication. Some people have no one at all, either because they are alone in life and the society they live in is uncongenial or indifferent, or because they themselves have withdrawn from the effort of making social contact, through timidity, lack of confidence or disappointment.

Levels B and C are where we talk about important and fairly confidential

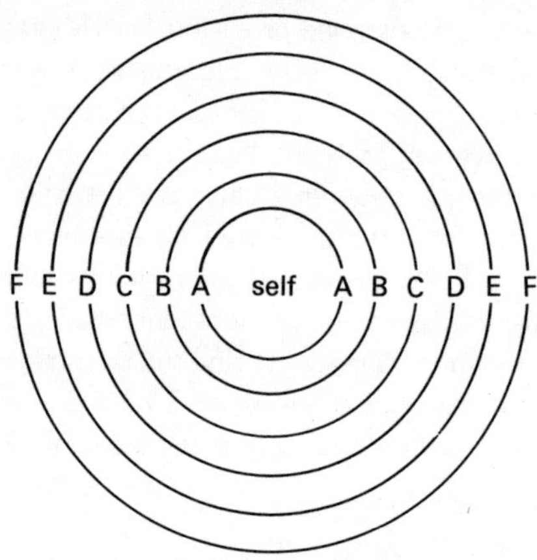


**Figure 7.2** *Your levels of relationship with those around you*

personal material, such as work and money problems, and levels D and E are where we deal with people regularly but casually, such as through shared work, hobbies and interests. You might feel you need more than six levels to accommodate the range of people you meet and know in your life. That's up to you to think about, but keep in mind that it's closeness and confidentiality that matter, not how often you see people, or how closely you are related, or how near you live to each other. Much level A communication is done between long-standing intimate friends by letter or telephone, and everyone must at some time have had the experience of meeting a stranger on a long train journey or on holiday and sharing with them confidential personal information not normally made accessible even to family and close friends. This is level A communication in a level F encounter; and it shows that level F is not where it all finishes, but is, in fact, where it all starts.

Self-image is the way you see yourself as a person, in life and in the world. It includes your own ideas of what kind of person you are, how well you relate to other people, how effectively you do your job at work and discharge your private roles as spouse or partner, parent, family member and citizen, and what form your hopes and plans for the future take. Someone with a poor self-image will have low self-esteem and a poor sense of self-worth. Your own personal self-image will not always coincide with the way other people see you. It may be that because of faulty or limited judgement they do not appreciate you as you are. It is also possible that there are things about yourself that you are unaware of, and feedback from other people could help you to develop greater self-awareness. It's a fine balance, between how far we go to please others and how far we insist on remaining what we see as our real selves. It is when there is a serious mismatch between our own self-image and others' image of us that we need to give some attention to why this discrepancy exists, and if anything needs to be done about it.

To support a personal self-image that we can own and feel confident with we need to experience what is called psychological mirroring. When we talk to someone close and share our ideas and feelings with them, we need to recognise our own image of our self in the image they have of us. We need to feel that the person sees us as we see our self, which is how we really are; and that their view of us is positive and affirmative. We should get this kind of psychological mirroring from our spouses or partners, as they should get theirs from us. Perhaps it is too much to expect it from our children, at least when they are younger. But whatever our life situation, we need to seek out and cultivate relationships with people who can give us this sense of empathetic understanding and affirmation; and sometimes friends outside the nuclear and extended family can be important sources of this.

Going back to you, as a person and a student, at level A in the middle of Figure 7.2, I hope you will agree that the people you need to join you there are those who will give you their moral and emotional support, their understanding and continuing interest, and perhaps a challenge now and again when you need it. A tall order? Maybe. But being unclear about what you want is a sure way of not getting sufficient sense of direction to ever find enough of anything. Knowing what you need and want is the point from which to start to realistically explore what is possible for you.

If you now think about the kind of personal material you would place in your own levels A to F, it will help you when you come to do the exercises at the end of this unit. Exercise 2 of Unit 1 might help you to put names on your levels. Decide if six levels are about right, or if you need more or could manage with fewer.

I now want to make three further suggestions about the deceptively simple Figure 7.2. The first is that your own self-image will change and develop as you progress through life, and the people who reinforce it now may not do so in 5, 10, 20 or 40 years' time, should you be lucky enough to arrive there. What this means is that you almost certainly will need more, or different, people at level A. You need to try, throughout life, to move promising people inwards from level F, or wherever you meet them, into and through levels E, D, C and B, ready for promotion into a level A relationship, if you and they want it and the opportunity arises.

The second thing to keep in mind is that you need at least some people in all six of your levels, with ideally enough space in your life for newcomers at all levels. You should also aim for some promotional throughput from the outer levels all the time. Some people will never make promotional material as friends, but will remain, quite happily for both of you, at levels E and D. However, once someone has moved through into level C or B, they are on the way up the promotional ladder towards greater closeness and, beyond a certain point in friendship, there is no going back to the D and E fringes again. The way is forward or out; and you should be prepared to move people out if they will not move forward, and replace them by others who will. This brings me to the third important thing; realising the importance of level F as a source of new relationships. People keep passing in and out of it all the time. It is your outer interface with the wider world. It is the place where you can make choices and initiate things, some of which will almost certainly end up at level A. Every new friend you make starts out as a stranger.

## EXERCISES ON BEING SELECTIVE ABOUT PEOPLE

**At the end of Unit 1 I asked you to set your life and career objectives and at the end of Unit 5 to set your higher education study course objectives. I'd now like to ask you to think about all the people you know and to be honest about how far they share these objectives; to identify your own 'objective-sharers' with a view to bringing them more closely into your life. Exercise 2 and Figure 2.2 of Unit 2 will help you to think where to start looking, and I suggest the bottom of the list first, with community and interest group contacts outside the home, and old and new friends outside the family as possible sources of affirmation and support. Respond to the following questions, and to any others of your own that you would like to set yourself, with people's names (initials will do, if you want to be discreet) and give them grades on the following scale:**

***Scale rating for closeness in objective-sharing*: very close (VC); fairly close (FC); impartial (IM); indifferent (IN); unsupportive (US).**

**a. Who shares my life objectives?
All of them? Some of them? Which of them?**
**b. Who shares my career objectives?
All of them? Some of them? Which of them?**
**c. Who shares my hobbies and recreational interests?
All of them? Some of them? Which of them?**

**d. Who shares my cultural and educational interests?**
**All of them? Some of them? Which of them?**
**e. Who shares my study objectives?**
**Already? Almost certainly would do? Might possibly do?**

**These questions draw on the balanced life idea in exercise 2 of Unit 1. If you want to give a numerical score take VC=9/10, FC=7/8, IM=5, IN=2/3 and US=0, but there is no final overall total. You just go on adding as many people as you can as you go along. Have a quiet think about how far your family fits in here.**

## UNIT 8. Devising Strategies

Before we leave the beginning sections of this book on starting out and moving in, it will be useful to look back briefly over the topics we have covered by way of preparation for your entry to the world of work and study, and to draw together the main supporting strands that you will need to hold on to as you progress. The skills that need to be emphasised are those of objective-setting, advance planning and negotiating and, if you have thought about the content of these units and worked your way through the exercises, you should be beginning to see that these are not just purpose-specific skills to be forgotten about as soon as you feel you are on the right track with what you want to do, but general purpose skills that should be made into lifelong habits so that you use them automatically as needed.

Objective-setting is something that needs to be done on short, medium and long-term time scales; daily, weekly, termly, yearly, and at intervals over the period of 5–10 years that you will be spending on getting the qualification you want. All objectives benefit from being written down and from being subjected to three constraints:

1. they should be *specific*; that is, clear, simple, to the point and about one thing at a time;
2. they should be *achievable*; that is, broken down into small steps that are do-able, rather than left as large tasks that may prove impossible;
3. they should be *measurable*; that is, you must be able to know when you have achieved your objective.

Unit 13 on time management will help you with setting short-term objectives to keep daily life ticking over, and we will look later on in this unit at setting longer-term objectives to act as staging posts as you move on along your chosen route.

Advance planning involves both time and the financial aspects of what you have decided to do. Much of your life will be dictated by arrangements other people make that you can do nothing about; whether it be the set hours and days of the normal working week, with your employer's restrictions on when you can take your holidays, or the equally restricting format of the academic year calendar. As a mature student you will need to be doubly aware of management needs, as you try to compress all you have to do into a restricted time limit and at the same time manage to make your money spin out until the end of it. Negotiating skills will be called for whenever you deal with people and arrangements, and you will gain most by exchanging benefits rather than by driving hard bargains. If family and friends are supportive of you now, make it clear that your support will be forthcoming for them whenever they want to do anything in the future.

## Can I plan out my route over the next five years?

You may need to draw up your own action plan calendar here, as most diaries and year planners cover only one or two years, and in any case you want to see everything at once on a single page. What you will need to mark in will be term dates and examination dates, if you are a full or part-time student, and later on to add submission dates for essays, projects and assignments as you go along. If you are a distance-learning or flexi-study student, your own up-to-date records of work completed and work yet to be done are specially important, as you will not have the regular reminder of having other students around you talking about what they have or haven't done yet, and when they have to do it by. The exercises at the end of this unit will help you to start to plan for yourself along these lines.

From a practical and professional point of view, the most important events on the calendar will be those dictated by work or study schedules. From a personal point of view, the most important parts of the calendar are the gaps, not ear-marked for work or study commitments but available for leisure, recreation and relationships. You should arrange to have some free space on your daily schedule each day, and on your weekly schedule at weekends, when you can take some exercise whether in or out of doors, spend some time on a recreational or cultural interest or a practical hobby, and make yourself available to your family and friends for just being together. You may well share some of your interests with family and friends, in which case you can do these things together as a way of being together.

The role of holidays in most people's lives is crucially important. A holiday is a time we set aside for ourselves, to recover from the tiredness and stress of working life and re-charge our batteries, and to recover a sense of perspective about what we are doing and where we are going in life. Some people like the stimulus of an active holiday, while others prefer a time of total relaxation free of any organised activity. If relationships are part of your life, they will be part of your holiday plans too, and the opportunity to be together and do things together with family and friends restores the balance and harmony of personal life, which can be so undermined and fragmented by the conflicting demands made on your personality elsewhere and the disorganised and chaotic conditions under which many people have to carry out their daily lives.

## What strategies shall I need to deal with personal problems?

The units in Section IV on keeping moving are designed to help you to avoid the problems that can arise from poor time management and from allowing fatigue and stress to take you over to the point where your general health becomes run down and your lack of energy becomes debilitating. There are also recommendations for avoiding crises as far as possible and surviving them and coping with them when you can't. We have looked at how to get the cooperation of your partner, family and friends in support of your plans for work or study, and how to ensure that damage to relationships is avoided by concentrating on being available regularly and predictably, even if it is sometimes only for short periods, to offer people quality time in which you give them your undivided attention and interest, and share whatever their current needs and concerns are.

We have concentrated so far largely on your immediate family, as they will be the people most directly concerned with the changes in arrangements necessitated by your return to work or study. But the very fact that they are so close can sometimes mean that they are the least capable of being objective about what is happening to you in your life and how you feel about it. What I want to ask you to do now is to start building up a personal contact network of relationships, of your own choice and for your own reasons, and getting it to work in such a way that it can offer you the measure of objectivity about problems and the moral support in getting solutions that the people closest to you in your daily life sometimes cannot. If they can, so much the better; it's a bonus. If they can't it ceases to be a cause of annoyance of frustration if there is someone else available who will.

I shall ask you to draw up your personal contact network at the end of this unit. You need to decide for yourself what you need from other people, using the list you draw up as your starting-point. Think about things like the kinds of jobs and careers that are represented, and how far people's work and study experience could be of help to you, if only by being understanding because they have gone through it themselves. Think about people's skills, interests and personalities, and try to break down your main list into sections, according to what individual people have to offer to you. Make contact with as many of them as you can, to sound out their level of interest in your plans, and decide who seems a good prospect for promotion out of level F into level B or C. When you have drawn up your network lists, leave room for the people you will meet as fellow-students or work colleagues, whatever their age. They are the people with whom you are going to share most, and upon whom you will need to rely greatly for day-to-day understanding and support. The 18-year-old you study with now will be touching 30 in 10 years time, and possibly having some of your problems themself, so there's room for growth.

## Do I really want to go on with all this?

This is the time to ask yourself this crucial question, both about your life plans and about this book. The beginning sections on starting out and moving in have set the background against which you will have to undertake your work or course of study, and have perhaps been a bit discouraging at times, because of the importance of not underestimating the problems. What I haven't tried to convey, because everyone has to experience it for themself, is the enormous intellectual and personal growth that comes from commitment to an academic discipline with all its demands, and the flowering of personality that accompanies prolonged and intimate contact with an academic subject that you come to love. Most people who choose their own subject of study find it the beginning of a lifelong interest, and for some it takes on the excitement of a lifelong love affair.

Before you decide whether or not to go on with whatever course of study you have been thinking about, it's a good idea to decide whether or not you really like the subject. There is a massive investment of life and resources in the years of an advanced study course, and in the process of making a commitment to one thing, you do of necessity have to give up others. If you love the subject you will not resent the demands and sacrifices; if you are half-hearted about it or indifferent to it you will. In thinking about this, it seems more and more to me as though I am talking about a marriage, and there are many similarities between having a committed relationship with an academic discipline and having one with a person. If you love the subject or the person, you can put up with the ups-and-downs, tolerate the eccentricities and irritations, bear the legitimate demands the situation makes of you, and shoulder responsibility for making the continuous effort of holding the relationship together and moving it forward. What happens ultimately is that you realise you are part of a partnership, and that it is the subject which is holding you together, mentally, emotionally and personally.

So, what I'd really like to say is, don't do a degree in a subject you don't like. It isn't worth it, it's a waste of life, and it can't possibly make you happy. However, if you do feel you'd like to carry on, for better or for worse, with whatever you've chosen to do, welcome to the following units of this book. Welcome to the rest of this book anyway. Even if you decide against advanced study there are parts of it that you will find useful, whatever you decide to do in life.

## EXERCISES ON PLANNING PERSONAL SUPPORT

**1. From Figure 5 in the exercise at the end of Unit 5 you will have a plan of how you aim to organise yourself on a year-by-year basis over the duration of your forthcoming study course. What I'm going to ask you to do here is to repeat the exercise in more detail for the next three years ahead, doing it for a year at a time, so that you've got a shorter timescale plan available for the near future. Make separate plans for each of the forthcoming three years and enter definite dates as you know them, pencilling in tentative dates that are still a long way ahead and not finally fixed. Keep these plans readily available in a folder, or even better, pinned on the wall of your study room or area, should you have one. As you move from the first one on to the second, start to fill in the details of the third and to draft a fourth one. Don't throw the first one away until it's at least a year out of date. You will probably find that you end up with your own five-year plans from which to organise your life and study. Don't forget to include time-out and holidays.**

**2. Using a large sheet of paper, list all the people who could become part of your personal contact network. Keeping in mind Exercise 2 of Unit 1, group them according to what they contribute to the balance, variety and richness of your life. You might like to include shared job and career interests, shared hobbies and recreational activities, and shared cultural and educational**

**interests. The group of people involved with you on your higher education study course will include tutors and fellow students and you can build this up as you go along. This should widen the range of people you have to draw on, if you now reconsider your responses to the exercises at the end of Unit 7. Put these, and any other questions important to you, to yourself in this way:**

**a. X is the name of a person. I find myself wanting to see more and more of X. What is it that X is offering me that other people aren't?**

**b. Y is the name of something I need in life that only a person can give.**
**Who can give me Y?**
**How can I get more Y from X?**

# III
# ACQUIRING SKILLS

## UNIT 9. Developing Expertise

There are some things that you will need to be able to do as a student that can be learned as techniques, such as note-taking during lectures, examination technique and the management of your own study time and personal resources to greatest effect. It is just a matter of learning the rules for how to do these things best, or of finding your own rules and having the persistence to apply them. There are other things, such as reading and writing for essays, assignments and research, that require much more of a student than just applying rules; they demand breadth and depth of subject knowledge and sophistication of understanding, to enable the student to work competently with their academic subject material and to do justice to it at the level of their present best ability.

The study skills which are a matter of technique need to be acquired straight away, as you will need most of them from the first day of your course. The study skills which require a developed understanding of your academic subject and depend on your ability to function in it competently can only be acquired over time. You will start to practise them from the beginning, but you will need much help by way of comment and criticism from your tutors and you should welcome this, as this is the part that you cannot just read up on your own but which does need experienced professional support and encouragement to develop. This is the way you should look at all tutorial criticism of your work: as something ultimately constructive which is part of your academic subject training, and without which you will never develop the competence and refinement of judgement to function effectively in your subject area.

All study skills reduce essentially to four basic competences: listening, speaking, reading and writing, and you will need to practise these constantly from the most basic beginner student level up to the academic sophistication of high level postgraduate study. They are all concerned with the communication of ideas, whether they are your own through speaking and writing, or those that other people impart to you when you read or listen attentively and sensitively. They are also concerned with the conveyance of factual information, so that as well as being articulate and literate, the modern educated person needs to be numerate, at least at a basic level. It is also inevitable today that students need to extend their skills to include computer literacy for the purposes of word-processing, computer-assisted learning and accessing databases for information.

## How well do I know how to listen?

You will need to be able to listen attentively and with concentration for periods of up to an hour continuously during formal lectures. You will also need at the same time to take notes summarising the main points of the lecturer's discourse for your own revision purposes later. You will need to be able to hear something said, to hold it mentally for long enough for your brain to process and understand it, to extract and write down your summary note of the essential point and, if appropriate, to decide whether you agree with it or not. If you don't agree, or if you don't understand, this is the point at which to say so; to give the speaker the chance to clear up any misunderstandings or to clarify the point they want to make. If you let things pass you can become hopelessly lost, and once you do raise a point of difficulty there are always other students who appreciate your initiative as they too have felt confused.

Your notes form the basis for your on-going learning and revision programme, and research shows that learning is more effective if material is revised at appropriate intervals. Immediately after a lecture your mind can be too swamped with detail and too much under stress to remember the lecture content very clearly. The amount you can remember improves over the next few hours and then declines quickly so that most of it is lost within 24 hours. If you can read through your notes later on during the day of the lecture it helps to top up what has slipped away from immediate memory and halt the decline. Research shows that other critical review periods occur at one week and one month after the initial presentation of new learning material, and also at three months and six months. If you can build in revision at these intervals as part of your study programme, your learning will become progressively easier.

## How shall I plan my study day?

You need to treat being a student as a job of work and to do at least an 8-hour day and a 40-hour week. If you are already working and your study is carried on entirely part-time your situation is completely different and you will have to plan carefully how you can extract the required number of study hours for your course from a crowded week. People vary in the time of day which finds them at their most alert in attention and concentration and you need to know when you are at your best mentally. If you are better able to work during the morning, do your more difficult work then, even if it means getting up as early as 5 or 6.00 am on two or three mornings a week and working before the rest of your household rises. It is a good time of the day for general peace and quiet and is only really difficult over three to four months in the depths of winter.

If you are a person who prefers to work at night, then rely on getting two to three hours later on after 10.00 pm when the rest of the household are either thinking about going to bed or settling into some quiet late-night leisure, watching TV or listening to music or the radio. Some people actually prefer to work during the night and it is up to you to decide what your optimum time is and how to get some of it for your more demanding intellectual work. More routine work can be done at times when your concentration is past its peak and it is a matter of time management and planning to do your best with your own mental resources.

Whatever time of day is best for you, you will also have your own personal concentration span, usually from 30–50 minutes depending on how exacting the study material is. If you intend to work for a two-hour slot, which is about the most useful long study period, go to your study place where you have your resources and work materials to hand and spend a few minutes collecting your thoughts and planning how you are going to use the time. Then settle down for however long you can work effectively without a break, say 30 minutes, and then stop deliberately and allow yourself to relax for a few minutes before continuing. It's a good idea to review quickly what you covered in the first 30 minutes before starting on the second 30 minutes. This gives an even transition from one block of work to the next and acts as a top-up to memory. Repeat this at the end of the second 30 minutes and then move into the last 30 minute block of your two-hour slot. Spend the last 10–15 minutes reviewing your work and then round it off and have a cup of tea or coffee, or at least reward yourself by doing something you like for a few minutes.

There does seem to be some decrease in memory with age, but it is relative to what the person's memory was like earlier in life and depends more on training than anything else. Younger people will have less to remember in general than older people and their recall for subject-specific detail will thus probably be better. They will also have fewer distractions than the person with family responsibilities, and the mature student can expect to make more of a conscious effort with memory tasks than probably the younger person needs to. The older student may also need to change the hours of their study day and do more earlier on while they are mentally and physically fresher, keeping evening slots for more routine study tasks. Travelling time and time between lectures can also be usefully employed for revision or background reading, and the student with a lot of commitments has to use all available time, whenever it is, letting nothing slip through their fingers.

## What kind of exam techniques shall I need?

Before you sit an examination you should know what to expect in terms of choice and range of questions and for how long you will be expected to write about each. Past papers are the best general guide to the format to expect, though the rubric of instructions at the head of the paper should always be carefully checked for any unexpected changes. If it is possible to know the allocation of marks to particular questions and parts of questions, it does help in planning your time. You can see from past papers which are the most popular topics and how frequently they are set, and you can make sure that you know these topics particularly well. If you can see that a topic you don't really like or feel confident in is likely to be examined, you must make an effort to get to grips with the material as you may be unable to avoid it other than by missing out a question.

If you have to answer five questions for which you can get 20 marks each, it is more important to make an average attempt at all of them and get, say (13 × 5) = 65 per cent, than to try to do two or three questions very well and make scratch efforts at the others. You are unlikely to get anywhere near 20 marks on any question, as this would be as good as saying that you have said the last word on the subject, which is never possible given the variety of opinions that exist on any academic subject. The first 10 marks are easy to get on a question that you know well, and the next 5 not so difficult, but the last few will always be an argument with the examiner and you will lose. So by all means prepare your favourite questions if you think they are going to come up, but be absolutely ruthless about the amount of time you spend on them, and remember that running over time on one question means losing time on the next.

It is important to understand the instructions given implicitly in a question about the kind of treatment that is wanted. Instructions such as *outline*, *indicate* and *summarise* are telling you to write briefly. Instructions such as *account for*, *analyse* and *explain* ask you to give reasons. *Interpret*, *assess*, *criticise* and *evaluate* ask you to form an opinion about something. These distinctions of meaning are important and you should recognise them from the occasions on which you have been asked to write essays along these lines.

The most important thing to remember about examinations is that you can only get marks for what is written down, not for what is in your head, so you have to write it down quickly and remorselessly. Don't worry about introductions or conclusions or refinements of writing style. Just write what you want to be read and what conveys your level of knowledge of the subject. Never obliterate draft notes on your question answer. Leave them where they can be seen and perhaps collect a few marks for you if you don't manage to write everything you want on a particular topic. Given a good subject knowledge, you can raise your examination mark by 10–15 per cent on exam technique alone, so that it is worth remembering a few essentials and putting them into practice when the time comes. Keep the question you are answering clearly in your head so that you are not sidetracked by irrelevant detail, however interesting; and try to leave yourself enough time at the end of writing to draw the strands finally together and form your conclusions.

## EXERCISES ON NOTE-TAKING

**Using an informative personal interview programme from radio or TV, take notes on the responses of the person being interviewed to the interviewer's questions and write up your notes later in the form of a short biographical essay (not more than 1,000 words). If you are using a longer programme, choose one with a leisured pace such as 'In the Psychiatrist's Chair', or 'Desert Island Discs' where you get a chance to rest while they play the music. Those of you who are sports fans might like to take notes as the radio announcer reads the football results. The faster pace will be offset by the fact that you will know the teams' names and be able to abbreviate them, and it will be interesting for you to see how much easier it is to take notes when you already have a background knowledge of the subject. Move on to note-taking from party political broadcasts or interviews when you can cope with evasion and deviousness without responding emotionally and losing concentration.**

# UNIT 10. Improving Communication

The interaction between learning and teaching to produce education is a two-way process and there is no role in it for passive acquisition of knowledge on the part of the student. As a student you must actively take responsibility for your own learning and deal with problems that arise just as you would with any other work or life problems. You will not be able to do much to change the teaching style of individual lecturers and it will really be up to you to adapt to that style and extract the benefits from it, minimising whatever problems there are. There are advantages and disadvantages in every teaching style and the more flexible you become the better it will serve your own interests as a student, and the better basis you will develop for understanding people and books as sources of information subsequently in life.

Recently, much thought has been given to research on brain functioning, and to the different ways in which the left and right halves of the brain interact with each other to process information and ideas. The left brain deals with logical and analytical thinking and handles most of language learning and performance. It looks at detail, at sequential and cause and effect relationships. The right brain takes an overview of all the information at its disposal and forms a holistic or unified view of what it all means when the individual parts are appropriately related together. The right brain is generally regarded as the source of artistic creativity and the left brain as the seat of rigour and intellectual discipline. The truth is probably more complex, but there is, in any case, a necessary place for both in learning.

It has been suggested that modern technological society places greatest emphasis on the logical and analytical left-brain style of thinking and tends to discount creative right-brain mental activity as inadequately grounded intuition. This is probably true to some extent, though it is more important in study to realise the potential and limitations of both and not to give one or the other inappropriate predominance in intellectual evaluation and decision-making – or in any other area of decision-making for that matter. The analytical breakdown of factual information, followed by a holistic overview of its significance, are intellectual activities which are just as much used in the concept-formation and problem-solving areas of science as they are in historical research, the appreciation of literature, or in the student's own production of good quality writing for essays or assignments.

## What is my style of learning?

Educational research on how brain hemisphere predominance affects learning style has identified four main learning approaches: the *practical* and *logical* approaches which draw much on left-brain activity and are at their most useful in subjects like mathematics, science and engineering; and the *imaginative* and *active* approaches which rely on right-brain holistic thinking and are needed for effective working in subjects like art, design and music. Older students in particular will probably have already acquired a learning style, from previous education or their work, and they may need to be prepared to go outside the range of their normal approach to work and study and see how these other learning approaches can help them to think and work better.

The person with the *practical* approach to learning is usually highly organised and works better alone; but they often take a narrow view of whatever they are asked to do and fail to see other people as helpful collaborators in generating new ideas. The person with the *logical* approach can similarly lean towards doing things in established ways and being too cautious in trying out new ideas. They also work better alone, or at least they think they do, because they fail to realise that social interaction and communication generate valuable opportunities for pooling intellectual resources and allowing greater creativity to emerge. They do have the strong points of being thorough and painstaking, both in achieving understanding and then applying it, but their left-brain mental functioning is too dominant, and allows insufficient scope for holistic thinking.

The *imaginative* person is good at seeing the connecting links between different areas of work and developing the overall concepts to accommodate them. They are innovative at coming up with new questions, new answers, new methods and new points of view about things. They can, however, be rather disorganised in practical ways and tend to work sporadically rather than consistently; they are organised in their own way and work at their own pace. Like their fellow right-brain thinkers the *active* learners, they are cooperative workers in groups and get much from exchanging ideas with others. The *active* learner is an intuitive, trial-and-error learner who is flexible and adaptable and doesn't mind taking risks and trying something totally new. They too are only selectively well-organised, and can readily take on too much work that they like doing at the expense of neglecting important things they feel less interested in. Both these learning styles would benefit from a bit of left-brain discipline, while losing nothing creative on the right-brain side.

If you find you do not take to a particular tutor's approach to lecturing or seminar work, it may well be that he or she has a learning and presentation style that is in strong contrast to your own, and it is extremely helpful if you can recognise this. People who are used to a highly disciplined approach to academic work find total immersion in right-brained intuition and creativity very uncomfortable and disconcerting, and it may get on their nerves to the point that they cannot learn effectively through it. The student who cannot adapt themself to what they feel is an alien approach may need to find another way of accessing this particular area of work, through their own reading from library books or by attendance at other sorts of lecture. Book authors similarly have different approaches and it is a matter of finding one whose approach suits you and your learning style. But don't give up your left-brained or right-brained teacher without an effort. They wouldn't be where they are now if there was nothing useful in their style.

## How can I think more effectively?

If you aim to achieve more effective communication in speech or writing, more effective thinking is a prerequisite. Whatever you want to say or write, you need to straighten it out in your head first. This is where the logical and analytical left-brain approach scores in organisation and attention to detail, but there is always a role for holistic right-brain thinking in maintaining an overview of what is happening and seeing alternative possibilities as they emerge in speech or writing. As a student you will need to think in your head as you read or listen, think on your feet as you respond to other people's ideas in discussion, and think on paper as you write essays, assignments or examinations. There is a role in all of this for both careful planning and a bit of creative inspiration.

The role of right-brain thinking is to maintain an overview of what is going on when you interact with other people in argument or discussion. It can look quickly at alternatives as other people present them to you or as you think of them yourself, and can look round the problem from different points of view and forward along the path the argument is taking. If you cling tightly to a rigid attitude because you don't want to be seen as a woolly thinker or someone who lacks confidence in their own ideas, you will let negative feelings inhibit your right-brain thinking and any free flow of creative ideas will stop. It's far better to take a risk that a spontaneous idea will not stand up to close examination later than to try to evaluate everything and its consequences so carefully that your ideas never get off the ground.

## How can I write more effectively?

When you are writing an essay or preparing your ideas in advance for discussion at a seminar, a popular right-brain approach is that of brainstorming. You take a sheet of paper and write your topic briefly in the middle of it, and then write down spontaneously and briefly any passing thoughts that occur to you on the subject over the next few minutes. How long you go on brainstorming your ideas is up to you, but you will sense for yourself when your mental resources are exhausted on that particular topic. You then go over your ideas and try to group them together where they appear related, cancelling out completely anything you think is not relevant for your present purpose. The aim of brainstorming is range and quantity, not quality. It is for the critical and analytical left brain to bring order and planning into this melting-pot of ideas as you go through them and see which ones can contribute usefully to the writing task you have.

Given that you understand the instruction form of an essay title, which tells you in what depth, breadth and detail to approach it and what kind of opinion, comment or conclusion you are expected to work towards, don't analyse the title in excessive detail. Just choose a line you would like to take and try to follow it through, first in note form as you work through your ideas from brainstorming and order them into the case you want to present, and then as a first essay draft, if you need one, before writing your final version. Some tutors like to see your notes and first draft, but do keep in mind that when you write under examination conditions your first draft will be your only draft and it is good practice to make the best possible job of this at first go.

Essay lengths can range from 1,200 words, through 2,500 words or 5,000 words, up to 10,000 words on a postgraduate dissertation. If you have prepared well by background reading and research, where necessary, to augment the basic subject coverage in lectures, you should be able to do the brainstorming and subsequent organisation quite quickly and fairly soon afterwards write the essay. With experience you should not need more than one session of about one to one and a half hours to write 1,200 words. You will have to do more than this in examination writing and will not then be able to concern yourself with the refinements of writing style and the conventions of essay format. Longer essays will need several sessions and you should follow general study advice about not working for too long without a break, and splitting up what you have to write into convenient length sections that can be completed over the course of a few days.

When you are writing a longer essay, however carefully you plan the line you are going to follow and the way you want to build your material around this, you will experience a constant interplay between the line you are trying to take and how this is affected by what emerges during writing. You will change your mind about what you think as you go along. During relaxed and confident writing the left brain holds the mental organisation together and coordinates your writing-hand movements, while the right brain is free to rove, re-appraise and review, often bringing out fresh ideas and different points of view that cause you to see your work in a new way. Take account of these insights, as this is holistic thinking. Check back regularly that you are answering the question or staying with the title as set, but don't decide about the end until you get there; your conclusions may be different from the ones you started out with.

### EXERCISES ON ESSAY-WRITING

**Choose a controversial essay title that stimulates your ideas but not your prejudices, brainstorm it and write it as a three-paragraph essay of not more than 500 words, or a six to ten paragraph essay of not more than 1,000 words. Build up the length of essay you can write to about 1,250 words in one and a half to two hours, including brainstorming and preparation in note form. Use this opportunity to check from your own handwriting how many words you write per line on average, and thus how many per A4 sheet of paper. This will help you in estimating essay lengths in future.**

**The exercises you have done for Units 9 and 10 will help to build up the abilities you need for *units of competence 7 and 8* in Figure 4.1 of Unit 4.**

## UNIT 11. Tapping Resources

A course of lectures on any subject can only give the essential bare bones of what a student needs to know. As a listener to a lecture course from which you are expected to take on massive amounts of new information at speed and under pressure, you will feel initially that even this is overpowering, but you will always find your lecturers impressing upon you that they are only giving you the basics and that more needs to be done. You will be given long book lists by every lecturer, and with luck they will make a personal recommendation of two or three books which form the backbone of the body of subject knowledge you are going to be expected to acquire. It is advisable to buy your own copies of basic books that the course of lectures is structured on, if they are at all affordable, as there is always tremendous pressure on library resources where popular books are concerned.

It is probably true to say that if you attend all your basic lectures and seminars, read the recommended course books thoroughly and are totally familiar with their content, and know your lecture notes by heart, you will pass your final examinations successfully. But this is only sufficient for basic borderline pass level, and to enhance your marks and raise your pass grade you need to show both breadth and depth of understanding of your subject and a growing competence in the way you function in it. If you are studying part-time or by distance-learning, under difficult conditions with only the minimum amount of time for study, you may have to settle for just knowing enough to pass, and to regard this as the major achievement that it is. But you must know this basic minimum amount properly and nothing less will be enough. Whatever else you can add from your own research and reading will only go to make things better.

## What resources are available within the college?

The main study resource for students in any educational establishment is the library, and you should get to know your college library, or libraries, as early as possible. Get to know the general physical layout and where the main subject sections are housed. Don't just think in terms of the specialism of your own subject – have a good look round at other things, particularly if you have other interests. A college, polytechnic or university library is the best collection of academic books that you will ever encounter, and it is yours for life if you become a graduate of that educational institution. You may also find, in the course of your studies, that you need occasionally to access reading material from a totally different subject area to give you a different insight into your own work. This is when a broad knowledge of your library collections, and of your librarians' special areas of competence and interest, will lead you quickly in the most useful direction of enquiry to take.

The book collections you need to be most familiar with are those relating to your own subject area, particularly important standard reference books that are part of your recommended course reading but too expensive for the average student to buy. Go through all the library volumes that are on your recommended reading list and, keeping in mind what was said in Unit 10 about analytic and imaginative styles of writing and presentation, pick out the ones you think you could learn from most readily. Learn how your library catalogues its books and how to access the catalogue through a manual index or computer database. The Dewey System of grouping books into subject areas between 000 and 990 is in most common use, and with your subject librarian's help, you will quickly locate and learn the classification numbers you are going to need most regularly. Find out the procedures for reserving, renewing and returning books, which books can be borrowed for one day, one week, one month or more, and which books are for reference only and cannot be taken out at all.

Another important section of the library you must make yourself familiar with is that devoted to the research journals of your own subject area. You will not be expected to read these regularly, but you will be expected to refer to them for recommended specialist articles on particular topics, and to access them to give a broad background and base to any research you do yourself. As part of your higher education course you can expect to be asked to do written assignments which require some consultation of research journals; if you are doing a practically-based course such as science or engineering there will be project work, which again needs to draw on existing research at its most up-to-date. Written assignments and practical projects, while not having the status of original research, do require you to work independently and arrive at your own results and conclusions. If particular research papers are important for you, or sections of particular reference text books for that matter, you are allowed to take photocopies of up to 10 per cent of any given book, and your library will have photocopying facilities on hand for a small charge.

## Do I need to read in different ways for different purposes?

When you need to do a lot of reading, as you undoubtedly will do on your higher education course, it's a good idea to be clear about the different ways in which you can read and in which it is appropriate to read different things. You will never be able to do enough reading, or all the recommended reading, so it's very important that what you can do is effective. Much emphasis has been placed on rapid reading techniques and they are always useful to have at your disposal. Subject areas such as education, sociology and politics, where a very great deal is written because the issues are of major importance to everyone in everyday life, cannot possibly be given detailed reading throughout, and rapid reading methods offer a way of giving a quick initial coverage and focusing in on the main points quickly. On the other hand, technical and scientific subjects need the most detailed and sequential attention, as one stage precisely follows and depends upon another, so that rapid reading would lead nowhere and be a waste of the student's time.

Skilful reading is both a left-brained and right-brained activity, and you need to be able to relax and allow your right brain to take a holistic overview to give global comprehension of a text, but at the same time to be alert enough for your left brain to focus in quickly on anything important, particularly if you are taking notes from the text. It is very useful to be aware of how you are reading and why, whether you are scanning a text for global comprehension, perhaps on an initial reading, or following through a sequential argument in detail to a logical conclusion. It is also useful to be able to vary your reading speed at will, as appropriate to your material and purpose, and to be aware when two or three quick readings of a text are more likely to be effective than a single, slow, laboured reading. You should avoid misdirected reading, when you concentrate attention inappropriately on less important things or get swamped by trying to read too much, and the other extreme of passive reading, when you plough through a text without realising that you are not really concentrating at all.

Keep careful notes of all reading references from books and journals. You need to know title, author, publisher, place and date of publication, as well as page and chapter numbers. When assessing a new book as source material, pay attention to the author's status and academic credibility, how recent a publication it is, and to the quality of the author's sources of reference and bibliography. Check quickly the dust-cover summary and list of contents and chapter headings. Decide how effective the presentation, organisation and illustrations are. Read quickly through the first and last chapters, and the first and last paragraphs of intervening chapters, for ease of style and subject competence. Good quality writing takes much control and discipline and highly competent academics are not necessarily good writers or communicators. The more competent and experienced you become in your own subject area, the more readily you will be able to skim-read a new book or text and assess its accessibility and usefulness to you in your work.

## What are my own on-going resources?

Once your course finishes and you leave your college, polytechnic or university you will be left alone with your high-level academic qualification and its associated body of skills and knowledge to make whatever use you can of them in personal and professional life. All qualifications date as time passes and knowledge progresses, but most particularly technical and scientific ones, and you will need and should expect to make some effort to keep abreast of current developments and current thinking in your subject area.

You will know by the end of your course what the main professional organisations are for people working in your subject field, and if you are an engineer or scientist you may already be a student member of one. Whether you are going to work now or later, or precisely in your own specialist field or not, join a professional organisation operating nationally so that you can receive a professional journal regularly, and participate in national conferences where possible and in local and regional branch activities as often as you can. Most professional subscriptions are allowable as expenses against income tax if you are working and most professional organisations offer a reduced rate for retired or non-active members or members who are temporarily unemployed. Your professional journal offers you up-to-date information on thinking and progress in your subject and information about courses, conferences and jobs. Your professional association and its activities offer you regular contact with your professional peers as colleagues, associates and friends. From this you can begin to set up and extend a very valuable professional and personal network of people of your own educational level with shared work interests. Once you leave a higher education establishment that level of day-to-day contact has gone, and unless you make the effort to revive it yourself in whatever ways you can, you will find yourself educationally and professionally isolated and separated from the sources of intellectual and personal growth that peer group contact brings. In fact, it is never too early to start thinking about what your appropriate professional organisations can do for you, particularly if you are a flexi-study or distance-learning student and the day-to-day peer group contact of a learning institution is not there. Student membership of a professional organisation is always available at a reduced subscription and can be a valuable source of support as a student and of professional contacts later when you come to start looking for jobs or enhanced career prospects.

It is important today for any practising professional person to try to update not only their knowledge but their qualifications, and to add to them and extend them as they progress or diversify in their chosen career. If you have to do this at your own expense, consider it an investment of money in yourself, enhancing and upgrading your quality as a professional person. There is much emphasis today on retraining women who have taken career breaks to have a family and bringing them back into the workforce. With consistent attention to maintaining professional skills and knowledge once they are acquired, there need be no great difficulty in retraining either men or women. Regular habits of study and reading become part of the pattern of living and what we started out struggling with as students we end up in later life doing much more easily and sensitively, because we ourselves have become more sensitive people in the educational process.

**EXERCISES ON READING**

**I'd like you to sort out for yourself from an informative daily newspaper two kinds of writing: factual reporting and informed comment. Factual reporting will just give you the information about exactly what has happened, and perhaps what is expected to happen next. Informed comment will assume that you are already conversant with the background issues and will discuss them and comment on them, assuming you know what the writer is talking about. I now want you to practise two different approaches to reading using newspaper articles of your own choice: extensive or repeated fast reading for global comprehension, and intensive or slower and more careful reading for detailed understanding.**

**I suggest that you choose two articles on the same subject, one written as factual reporting and the other as informed comment. Deal with each one in turn and take a break between them. Take the informed comment article and read it quickly three times. Then put it aside and try to write down the main points from memory. Repeat this with the factual information article and see for which one global comprehension reading is most effective. Now read both in more careful detail, taking notes if you wish, to get practice in note-taking from texts as well as from listening. Decide if you think detailed reading, and the time it takes, is more necessary for one kind of text than the other.**

## UNIT 12. Asserting Competence

Much of the most productive holistic thinking is done through the interactive processes of group work in tutorials and seminars. A number of well-informed and intelligent people who have prepared their topic background carefully will be able between them to pool more ideas than any one individual alone. They will not only produce more ideas through working together but will modify each others' ideas and produce enough interactive stimulation to prompt the generation of fresh ideas. With the overall guidance of a tutor experienced in working in this way, the group will work towards a broader, more positive and higher level of consensus than any one or two individuals could reach working alone. This is the most disciplined kind of brainstorming, in which people use their logical and analytical faculties to vet their own ideas as they go along, and the tutor supplies an impetus or applies the brake to keep the activity channelled into forward movement.

If you have been used to a more role-defined style of working, where a lecturer or programme-presenter gives all the input in an organised and prepared way, and you as a student listener or viewer are merely asked to listen sensitively, take notes and perhaps ask a few specific and carefully phrased questions, you could find interactive group work a bit alarming at first. But you do need to make an effort to get over this, as you will be expected to participate in tutorial and seminar discussions in which the overall framework is deliberately looser, so as to facilitate individual contributions, interpersonal interactions and the holistic development of the group process. The only defined role is that of the tutor, who stops things running out of control and guides the group forward to whatever consensus of ideas and opinions it is going to reach.

## Can I assert myself in argument?

Assertion in interpersonal or group situations and in relationships is about reaching a negotiated balance when people have different ideas about what they think or what they want. It means that you respect yourself and your own ideas and wishes to the same extent that you respect other people and their ideas and wishes, in situations where you need to, have to or want to deal with each other. If you are the kind of person, man or woman, who has always thought that it was their role in life to take decisions for other people, or if you are the kind of person who has always allowed other people to take decisions for you, you will find the balance of assertion difficult to achieve at first, and you will need to develop the personal quality of assertiveness in order to negotiate it.

An assertive person has their own personal territory of ideas and action within moral, social and personal boundaries that they have worked out and set for themself. They do not expect other people to encroach on the autonomy of this territory without consent and would not expect to move into other people's territory without agreement. We need to observe respect for each others' independence of thought and autonomy of action, while at the same time remaining engaged in the process and effort of achieving mutual understanding through sharing of ideas rather than disengaged detachment.

When people are working together in a group the stimulus of interacting with each other will bring out a wide range of ideas, some of them strong or even controversial and all of them backed up by individual levels of enthusiasm, commitment and conviction. It is against the background of this complex interplay of ideas and their associated clashes of interacting feelings that you as an individual student will have to listen to and evaluate other people's opinions, formulate your own ideas and responses, have the confidence to articulate your personal thoughts and opinions, and to insist that they are heard and regarded and not by-passed or discounted.

There are some recognisable gender differences in the way people conduct themselves in interactive discussion groups, though it has to be admitted that there are lazily passive and disturbingly over-assertive people of both sexes. Men are used to taking action and being expected to have their own ideas and to stand up for them. Women often try to mitigate men's extremes and to reach working compromises, though sometimes at the expense of being over-adaptive and not holding out for enough of their own ground. It is the individual responsibility of each person to have something to say and to contribute it to the discussion.

## Can I put forward a convincing case?

It will sometimes happen that a tutor will ask individual students to take it in turn to present a tutorial topic, based on their own thinking and background reading round the subject. This can be quite a test of nerve and confidence for a student who has never done it before, but it gives the student an enormous boost to self-confidence to carry this through successfully with their academic and professional peers as an audience. In preparing what you intend to say, make what you see as a few main points, briefly and clearly, with supporting reasons and academic references where necessary. Do not be in any way apologetic for yourself or your efforts. Just trust your own judgement and plunge straight in to what you have to say. There is nothing more irritating at the beginning of a discourse than a speaker who keeps apologising for being there. Do not constantly refer to your tutor for approval or guidance. He or she will come in at the appropriate time with clarification or information as needed.

People have different styles of speaking to suit different occasions, ranging from formal, through informal, to downright casual, and most of us vary our speaking style appropriately without being aware of it. Where you do need to be more aware of how you express yourself is when you are writing for academic purposes, things like formal essays or technical and scientific laboratory and research reports. There is an accepted formal style with its own grammatical features and the vocabulary of the subject area, and to deviate from this leaves an unacceptable bad impression. It is like trying to function as a senior business manager without being able to write a proper business letter. If you do not know the difference between passive and active sentence constructions, buy yourself a basic English grammar and work through it on your own until you do, getting help or advice from someone competent if needed.

It is also important to realise that we use a different range of vocabulary, and different levels of vocabulary, for different purposes. All of us know words from reading that we would not use ourselves in writing or speaking, because we have never needed them often enough to move them from our passive vocabulary store into our active one. We all use words and styles in writing that we would rarely use in speaking, because speaking demands an economy and directness that has little time for conventional formality; and it has in fact conventions of its own. In writing this book I have not taken a formal style, because I have tried to address you person-to-person, and in doing so I have taken on more of the characteristics of informal speech, with its non-rigorous grammar and non-standard features of sentence presentation, than would be acceptable in formal academic writing. It's more a matter of being aware of what you are doing and when it is appropriate than of living with unbreakable rules.

## Do I need to do some work on my image?

In Unit 7 we looked in some detail at the idea of self-image and how it can be affirmed and enhanced by psychological mirroring from the right people. Someone's self-image can also be damaged and reduced by the destructive effects of being seen for too long and by too many people as a mediocrity or a nonentity. It is far too easy for the routine familiarity of daily life to reduce any of us to getting stuck in an image rut at home or at work. We are seen as exponents of fixed roles and not as the diverse and flexible individuals we are. Women who have spent years in domestic life coping with fractious children and tired men, and men who have spent years in routine and solitary jobs or surrounded by uncongenial colleagues, will find their own personality so drained and run down by lack of stimulation and positive input that their self-confidence and self-image are at a very low ebb.

When older mature people come back into higher education they can feel swamped by what is almost a culture shock when they encounter the energy, vitality and intellectual acuteness of younger people. The mature student needs to realise that they can tap into some of this energy and enthusiasm for life if they merge with and participate in the group life that they are here to share. Their own mental and emotional energy level will rise and they will be able to demonstrate the same motivation, confidence and commitment as their younger course colleagues. Maintaining a profile, creating an impression and keeping yourself on view are not only good public relations exercises with the people who will ultimately decide the value of your academic efforts, but good practice for the time when you will be looking for a job, and as ways of letting your bosses know that you are there and that your efforts are of value to them when you have a job. The confident self-image you develop as a successful mature student will make you a winner, not just now but for the rest of your life and career.

## EXERCISES ON IMPROVING ORAL SKILLS

**1. Think about the dynamics of typical discussions in which you have to participate as a student. If ten people are talking together for 60 minutes, that gives them five or six minutes each; probably five or six contributions of one minute each. If there are only five people, they will be able to speak for twice as long, and in fact will have to do so to keep things going. They will probably choose to speak twice as often, say 10 or 12 times in an hour, rather than speak for longer periods when they do contribute. If any one person speaks for longer than their total allocated time in an hour, someone else will lose part of their speaking time. If this is a recurrent problem in groups in which you participate, it can only be dealt with by members deciding together to control it, having their own contributions ready and being insistent on getting them heard. It is useless a tutor silencing an individual to create gaps in discussion if no one offers anything to fill them. For the seminars and discussion groups you attend, work out your allocated speaking time during an hour and make a point of having something to say, however brief, on the number of occasions on which you should be expected to speak.**

**2. Think about your own use of vocabulary and styles of expression, and how they differ for writing and speaking. Be aware of words you know from reading but do not use in writing or speaking, and of words you use in writing but don't normally have occasion to use in speaking. If your writing vocabulary is limited you need to read more. If your speaking vocabulary is very restricted you need to talk more to a wider range of educated people.**

**The exercises you have done for Units 11 and 12 will help build up the abilities you need for *unit of competence 8* in Figure 4.1 of Unit 4.**

# IV
# KEEPING MOVING

## UNIT 13. Managing Time

The most important thing about managing your time effectively is to find out exactly where it goes and make precise plans to re-organise it in more suitable ways. Any expenditure of our time that we make during the day can be regarded as either *discretionary*, where we have a genuine choice about whether to do something or not, or *non-discretionary*, where we don't have any option, certain things just have to be done. Non-discretionary time breaks down further into *paid time*, when we are contracted to an employer, or equally strongly committed to a voluntary organisation which relies on us absolutely, and *maintenance time*, when we have no choice but to do the necessary things at home to keep life ticking over for ourselves and others who depend on us.

### Where does my time go?

The first thing that you need to do is to fill in your personal time investment chart over a period of a week. This is done in Figure 13.1 for someone with a very simple lifestyle, and we suggest that you use this diagram as a basis for building up your own plan, showing weekday and weekend time planning.

The weekday timetable for this person shows this approximate breakdown:

| | *hours* | *% of day* | |
|---|---|---|---|
| Work and travel | 10 | 41 | |
| Sleep | 8 | 33 | } 42 |
| Maintenance | 2 | 9 | |
| Leisure | 4 | 17 | |
| | 24 | 100 | |

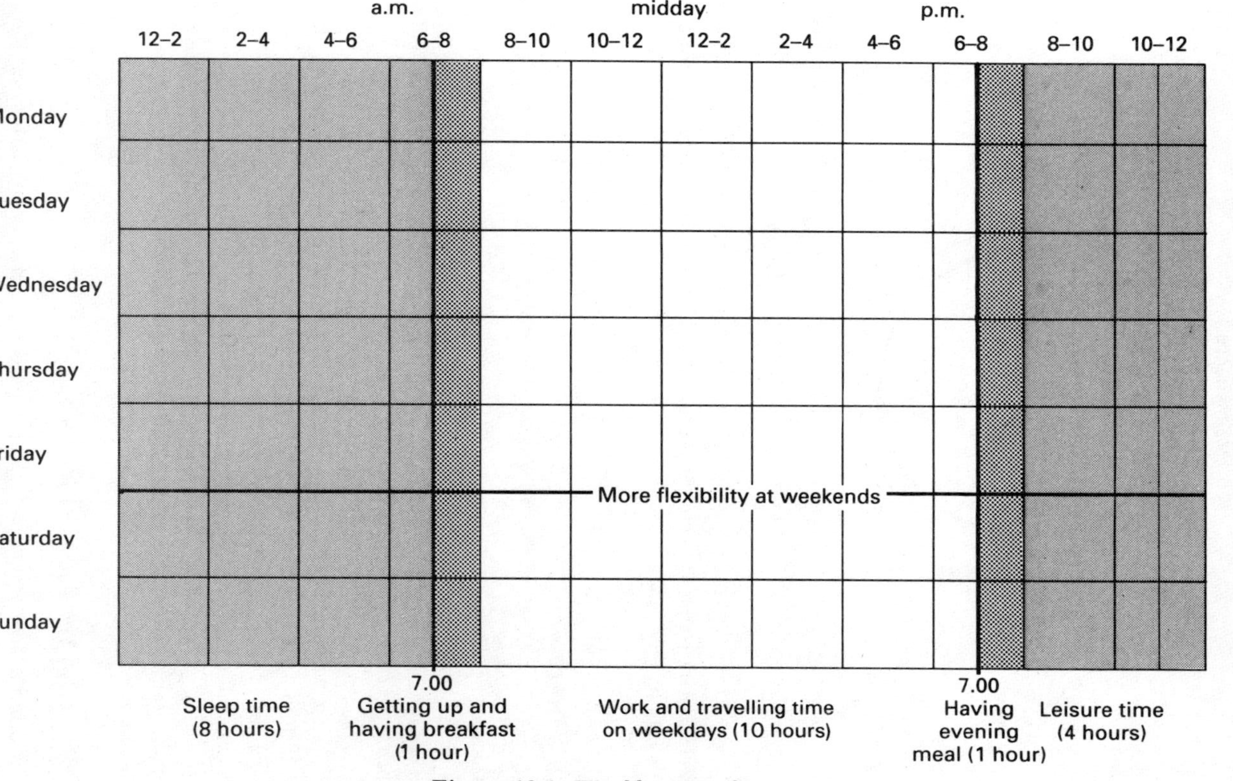


Figure 13.1 *Weekly time-planner*

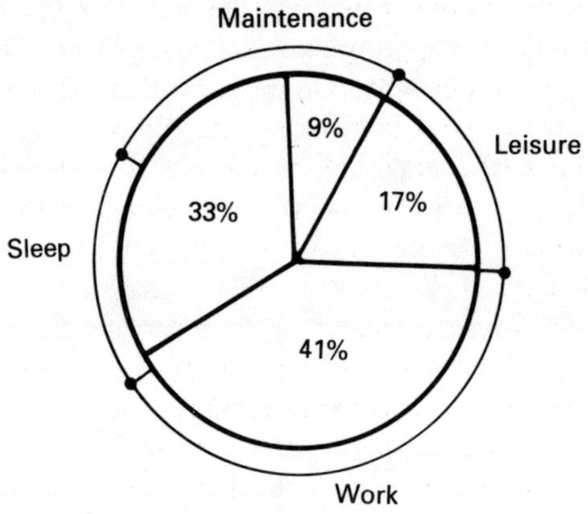


**Figure 13.2** *Percentage time allocation*

Research into what working people find to be acceptable limits for their time allocations shows:

| *Work* | *Support/maintenance* | *Leisure* |
|---|---|---|
| 25–30% | 45–55%<br>(30% of this should be sleep) | 20–25% |

Comparing this with the pie-chart (Figure 13.2), we can see that for even a simple lifestyle work can start to take over leisure time, and for someone with a heavy daily schedule of household and family duties not even weekends will bring clear enough periods of relief.

The person with the pie-chart lifestyle also clearly has no shopping, cooking, washing or cleaning to do. This is either done by someone else, or left until the weekend when it encroaches on precious leisure time then.

The person living alone and looking after themself, and the person who works full-time and looks after a family, will probably find that two to three of their evening leisure hours will vanish, and all they will have time for is a bath, and perhaps an evening drink or an hour in front of the television, before rolling into bed and the all-too-soon start of the next day.

## How can I get better time flexibility?

How much sleep you need depends on how good that sleep is. Many people sleep two to three hours longer than they need to, and still wake feeling tired and unrefreshed. Effective mental and physical relaxation is essential, both during our sleep and at appropriate times during our waking life. We shall look at what can be done to help in the section on stress management.

The other major help in reducing non-discretionary time is advance planning and regular routines. Make the decision to deal with major time-consuming activities such as shopping, cooking, washing, ironing and cleaning, in the least possible amount of time and as infrequently as you can get away with. Don't do jobs twice-weekly when once-weekly will do. Spend as much time thinking about what you plan to buy and cook as you do running around the shops or the supermarket going frantic for ideas. Do things on the same day every week, and at the same point in your daily routine, so that you have to do the minimum amount of thinking-out of regular activities and are mentally freer to plan ahead for things that need more concentration.

Wherever possible get help with a busy schedule. Spouses or partners can share in planning and helping with domestic routines. It is good that they do so, as many adults sooner or later find themselves alone for shorter or longer periods of their lives, often needing to look after children as well as work, and what this takes comes as a great shock to the person who has never tackled it before. All school-age children, and particularly teenagers, can learn to help and share responsibility for running a household. Many young people live away from home for considerable periods, for work or study purposes, and need the preparation for budgeting, planning and domestic organisation that life in a sharing family can give. The value of paid help should never be overlooked. Any person who works full-time should not feel that it is an indulgence to employ a cleaner or home-help. Having this basic chore dealt with regularly can remove a major source of worry for any working man or woman, and it is a way for the employed better-off person to help to redistribute their income to someone else, who may for whatever reasons be unable to get or accept alternative work.

It's also important to realise which of our support and maintenance activities we actually find enjoyable and relaxing, and could if we decided choose to regard as leisure. Some people genuinely love gardening while for others it's just another chore. Decorating the house and doing routine car maintenance are other things that some find a bore and others a challenge. Where we can assert a choice over whether something is support/maintenance activity or leisure we should try to treat it as leisure, as this is often really the only area that is time-negotiable for busy and heavily committed people. Women are particularly good at treating having a bath, and preparing to go out or go to bed in a leisurely way, as a form of relaxation, and often use it as an occasion for pampering themselves. This is not an indulgence, or a waste of time and money, but a way of giving ourselves some of the appreciation and attention that is often lacking in the rest of a busy life. People who tend to use cigarettes and alcohol as relaxants could well try this instead.

There must, for everyone, be some part of the day that is theirs and theirs alone because, if we carry on for too long being totally available to other people and constantly involved in their problems, we lose our own sense of personal identity and worth and begin to lack self-esteem. We need time for our friends, who give us an input rather than requiring an output from us all the time. We need time for our own hobbies and interests, and the mental renewal they give us. We need time for doing something we just want to do, whether other people think it's useful or not. And we need time, however briefly, for simply doing nothing, but just being, and experiencing ourselves as ourselves, alone if we need to be.

## How should a student manage the day?

Whoever you are, whether man or woman, if you are living with other people, particularly your family, you will have to get them used to the idea that you are not available 24 hours a day, but that at certain times you will be out attending classes or working in the library, and that some of the time you are at home will have to be devoted to study. This needs clear explanation, discussion and negotiation at the beginning, and considerable determination to follow through for however long your study course lasts.

Whether you are doing a short refresher course for a few hours a week, with a view to going back to work or on to further study, or a fully committed degree course over three to four years, the problem of staking a claim to the study time you need as your own needs to be dealt with in the same way. You need to have a clearly detailed schedule of arrangements written down where everyone who needs to know them can see them, and you need to tell people when you *will* be available to spend time with them talking through problems, or just talking, and when you *will not* be available for odd-jobbing, handy-manning, repairing bikes or shirts, or doing anything other than deal with your study assignments or absolute emergencies. The people you live with must get used to your routines and make them their routines, so that you get the mental and physical space for study and academic work and the support of a background routine that facilitates it.

As well as the time investment plan for your day and week, you can use the system of making lists, daily and weekly, to order priorities on a short-term basis. Some people like to list things they *must do*, things they *should do* (all being well) and things they would *like to do* (circumstances permitting). Other people just write everything down and then sort the items into A (top), B (middle) and C (low) priority order. If commitments are very pressing, re-sort Bs into As and Cs, put Cs aside, and then deal with As in order of priority. This listing is a useful exercise, but it needs daily review, as today's Cs can become tomorrow's As or Bs; or they can become irrelevant and be thrown in the dustbin. Business management consultants like to look at time as a bank which credits us daily with 24 hours, 1,440 minutes or 86,400 seconds. You can't keep anything in your account, there is no carry-over balance from day to day, and you can't borrow anything in advance. You just have to use up everything you've got as it happens, and you have to forget about what you've lost or missed.

## EXERCISES ON PLANNING YOUR TIME

**1. Complete your personal time investment chart for one week based on the ideas of Figure 13.1.**

**2. Identify:**

| | |
|---|---|
| **a) non-discretionary committed time (work or study)** | **hrs** |
| **b) non-discretionary support and maintenance time (including sleep)** | **hrs** |
| **c) discretionary leisure time** | **hrs** |
| **Total for week:** | **168 hrs** |

**Compare them with the figures for acceptable limits and, if you find it helpful, make your own pie chart. Think about how you could draw clearer boundaries for (c).**

**3. Write down at what point in the day, and for how long, you intend to find the following:**

**a) time for friends;**
**b) time for exercise;**
**c) time for doing something you enjoy;**
**d) time for doing nothing.**

**If you can't do this for a day, do it for a week.**

4. **List your top ten time-wasters in life.**
   **Are they things or people? Which of them are self-imposed and which are imposed by others?**
   **Decide to eliminate five of them. Of the remaining five, choose two or three that you will leave alone, because for you they are relaxing and you enjoy them as luxuries.**
5. **Write down three things you are going to do this week to improve your personal time-management.**
   **Write down another two or three things that you intend to do during the next six months to improve time-management.**

# UNIT 14. Managing Stress

When animals are confronted with a threatening or alarming situation their response is instantaneous: fight or flight. Which they do depends on their own perception of the situation. If they feel they stand a good chance they fight; if they see their chances are poor they escape at once. Both responses require the rapid mobilization of energy and physical resources, and the resulting build-up of stress response chemicals in the animal's bloodstream is dispersed naturally during the fight or flight activity.

Human beings also respond to a threat or confrontation by producing a build-up of stress response chemicals in the body, but the need for physical fight or flight has gone (except, of course, when we are threatened by an attacker or other physical danger), and we are left with all the distressing symptoms of anxiety and fear and no prompt way of getting rid of them.

## What are stressors?

Any people, things or situations that give us feelings of fear, anxiety or loss of control act as stressors and, if we can neither resolve the problem nor get away from it, we soon begin to experience ourselves as being under strain.

The Holmes-Rahe scale of stress ratings is one major piece of research in the area of individual stressful events, as experienced by one group of people over a period of two years in their lives. Complete the exercise in Figure 14.1 for the past two years of your life and find what your own score is.

A total score of more than 300 units corresponds to an 80 per cent chance of a serious change in your health condition within the next year. Exactly what the change would be depends on the individual's weakest link, however healthy they are in other ways. A score of less than 150 units reduces the chance of health change to 30 per cent, a score from 150–300 units gives a 50

| LIFE EVENT | VALUE | YOUR SCORE |
|---|---|---|
| Death of spouse | 100 | |
| Divorce | 73 | |
| Marital separation | 65 | |
| Jail term | 63 | |
| Death of a close family member | 63 | |
| Personal injury or illness | 53 | |
| Marriage | 50 | |
| Fired at work | 47 | |
| Marital reconciliation | 45 | |
| Retirement | 45 | |
| Change in health of family member | 44 | |
| Pregnancy | 40 | |
| Sex difficulties | 39 | |
| Gain of new family member | 39 | |
| Business adjustment | 39 | |
| Change in financial state | 38 | |
| Death of a close friend | 37 | |
| Change to different line of work | 36 | |
| Change in number of arguments with spouse | 35 | |
| Mortgage over one year's net salary | 31 | |
| Foreclosure of mortgage or loan | 30 | |
| Change in responsibilities at work | 29 | |
| Son or daughter leaving home | 29 | |
| Trouble with in-laws | 29 | |
| Outstanding personal achievement | 28 | |
| Spouse begins or stops work | 26 | |

| LIFE EVENT | VALUE | YOUR SCORE |
|---|---|---|
| Begin or end school | 26 | |
| Change in living conditions | 25 | |
| Revision of personal habits | 24 | |
| Trouble with boss | 23 | |
| Change in work hours or conditions | 20 | |
| Change in residence | 20 | |
| Change in schools | 20 | |
| Change in recreation | 19 | |
| Change in church activities | 19 | |
| Change in social activities | 18 | |
| Mortgage or loan less than one year's net salary | 17 | |
| Change in sleeping habits | 16 | |
| Change in number of family get-togethers | 15 | |
| Change in eating habits | 15 | |
| Holiday | 13 | |
| Christmas | 12 | |
| Minor violations of the law | 11 | |
| Misc: (give own score) | | |
| ______________________ | | |
| ______________________ | | |
| **Enter your total here** | | |

Score an event twice (or more) if it happens twice (or more).
If your total is over 300, then you have an *80 per cent chance of a serious change in your health within the next year.*

**Figure 14.1** *The Stress of Major Life Events*

per cent chance. Two other features of this research are that 20 per cent of the people with scores over 300 are not apparently troubled by stress but rather find it a stimulant and that, at the other extreme, a very low score is not good, as the person is under-stimulated and will find boredom stressful. This is the phenomenon of 'rust-out' as opposed to the better known one of 'burn-out'. Most of the events on the Holmes-Rahe scale clearly involve serious changes in a life or work situation, and it's best to avoid too many of these occurring together, if possible.

## How can you tell you've got stress?

There are commonly recognised physical, mental, emotional and behavioural symptoms of stress.

*Physiological stress* shows in headaches, back and shoulder tension, disturbed breathing patterns, skin irritation and rashes, digestive disturbances, tiredness due to poor sleeping patterns, and susceptibility to repeated infections due to running down of the body's immune system.

*Mental stress* shows in forgetfulness, poor concentration, disturbing dreams, persistent negative thinking, obsessional thinking, muddled and confused thinking, making frequent mistakes, persistent worrying, and frenetic and over-active mental states, alternating with feeling flat and passive, and leading to eventual exhaustion.

*Emotional stress* shows in feelings of nervous tension and anxiety, irritability with people and routine things, feeling threatened or alienated, depression and sadness, loss of energy and enthusiasm, loss of confidence and self-esteem, and general demotivation and loss of satisfaction in life and work.

*Behavioural stress* shows in increased drinking and smoking, compulsive activities such as gambling, disturbed sleeping patterns, loss of interest in relationships and withdrawal from people, putting up barriers with people and pretending things are ok when they are not, over-working and not drawing boundaries between work and personal life, poor time management and low productivity, feeling unable to relax and unwind, and general behaviour deterioration into counter-productive and anti-social behaviour when we make excessive demands on other people's time and understanding, but expect them to show patience and consideration to us however difficult to please and help we are.

Three stages of stress have been recognised; they are shown in Figure 14.2. *Stage I stress* is experienced as feeling under pressure. *Stage II stress* is experienced as feeling under stress rather than just under temporary pressure. *Stage III stress* is where the immediate threat to health arises.

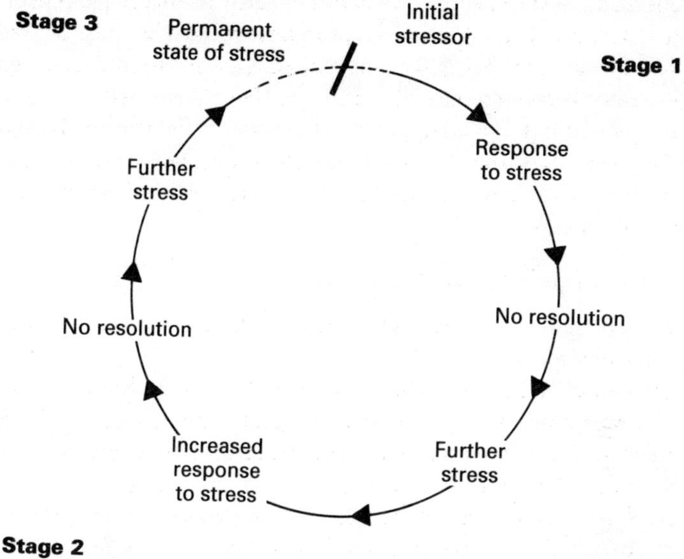


Figure 14.2 *Three stages of stress*

## What can you do about stress?

Prevention of stress where possible, and management of stress where it has to be tolerated, are the main strategies here. Research shows that personal performance is at its best between the extremes of 'burn-out' or excessive stress and 'rust-out' or under-stimulation. It is up to the individual to decide where peak performance is for them (see Figure 14.3).

A basic background of physical good health is essential to stress management. This means sufficient sleep and relaxation, a good basic diet and a suitable exercise programme. Many general medical practices now have a diet and lifestyle counsellor and it is worthwhile making an appointment for a routine check-up on weight and suitability of diet. Too many convenience foods, foods with high fat, sugar or salt content, and foods lacking in dietary fibre can undermine general health. Excessive tea, coffee and alcohol used as stimulants do not take the place of good quality energy-generating foods in your diet. Your food intake in calories should be sufficient to meet the energy requirements of your daily life and exercise routines; too little intake and you

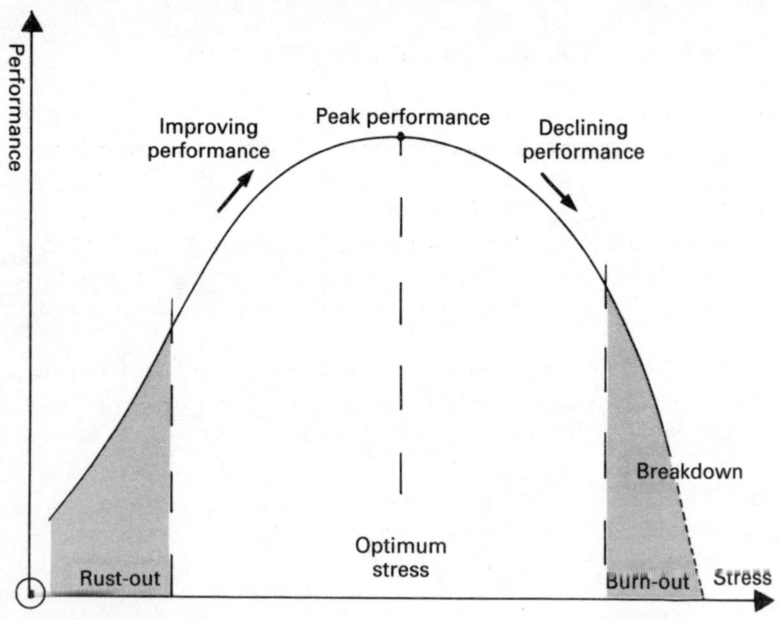


Figure 14.3 *Peak performance*

won't have enough energy, too much and you will steadily become overweight.

Most people have their own favourite way of relaxing, whether it is luxuriating in a hot bath or doing a relaxation routine. You need to find what is effective for you and build it into your daily programme. However busy they are, everyone needs to give themself half an hour a day that is their own, and their partner and family need to understand this. A parent with younger children may find it easier to arrange to go out for an evening a week, to a relaxation class or just to meet friends, rather than keep trying unsuccessfully to get a few hours peace at home. Getting this essential space for yourself is particularly difficult for women with families, but it does need to be negotiated with whoever you live with, or to be invested in financially by hiring a child-minder if you are a single parent, or by mutual exchange of child-minding services if money is very short.

There are many excellent books on stress management and the names of some of them are given in the Additional Reading section at the end of this book. But the major thing is to actually do something, on a regular daily basis, rather than just read about it, talk about it or think about it.

## EXERCISES ON COPING WITH STRESS

**1a. Complete the Holmes-Rahe chart and assess your score. Are there any major sources of stress for you that the chart leaves out?**

**1b. Read through the physiological, mental, emotional and behavioural symptoms of stress, and tick off any that you already have. Repeat this in six months' time after you have followed a stress management programme and compare the results.**

**2a. Decide where you think you are on the stress/performance graph. What would any extra stress do to you now? Which part of the curve would it push you onto? Would that be bad or good?**

**2b. List your main stressors in life.**
**Are they things, people or situations?**
**Which of them are self-imposed and which are imposed by others?**
**Choose two stressors you can do something about now and work on them over the next week.**
**Choose two or three more that you feel you could do something about over the next six months and start to plan them out of your life.**

**2c. What is going to happen to you eventually if you do nothing about these stressors?**

**3a. What do you do to wind down i) at the end of the day, ii) at the end of the week?**
**Is this effective enough for you, or do you need something else as well/instead? (If so, what? And what are you going to do about it?)**

**3b. How do you re-charge your batteries on holiday?**
**Is this enough, or do you need something else? (If so, what? And what are you going to do about it?)**

**4. Choose *one* stressor you can't do much about. How would you really like things to be? Would someone else in your situation insist on changing things? What toll is it taking of you leaving things as they are? Could you get support for change from anyone else? Is a fundamental review of your situation needed? What's the first step to take? Can you do it?**

# UNIT 15. Conserving Energy

It's probably much easier to recognise when energy is missing than to realise when it is there and where it comes from. Teenagers and adolescents seem to have enormous amounts of physical energy for things they are interested in doing, and often collapse into inertia when there is nothing going on to stimulate their interest. Energy is a much more scarce and valuable commodity for older people, because so much of it is spoken for, both inside the home and outside it at work, before we even get to thinking about what our hobbies and interests are. As well as being physically exhausted sometimes, most people would recognise the feelings of being nervously, mentally or emotionally drained. These are ways of having our resources run down for which just physical rest and enough of the right kind of food will be insufficient to bring about recovery.

## Where does energy come from and what drains it away?

You can be mentally tired from too much reading and study without a break, or from too much demanding thinking and decision-making. A change of activity to something practical or some physical exercise is usually of more use than sleep or inactive rest, which might not be very effective anyway until the mind has changed down gear into relaxation. Nervous exhaustion follows prolonged periods of having to remain alert and responsive to conflict or crisis, and having the decision-making part of your personality constantly on the line. Students of all ages will recognise this in the collapse into exhausted anti-climax that occurs when a stressful set of exams is finally completed. Emotional drainage happens when someone has to spend too much of their time and energy meeting other people's needs and dealing with other people's problems and feelings, at the expense of neglecting themself and their own life. This is typical of what can happen when someone is looking after other people who cannot do the normal amount for themselves, such as children, elderly infirm people and anyone of any age who is sick, whether temporarily or chronically.

I have avoided drawing outdated distinctions between men's and women's work because modern society is too complex and varied to fit into a framework of understanding that might have applied even as little as 30 years ago. There are men as well as women bringing up children on their own, or looking after an elderly infirm parent or a chronically sick spouse. Because they are fewer in number they are not less important, and the toll on their health and nerves is not less serious at an individual level. Their social isolation may in fact be greater, because men's traditional sources of support and friendship have often been outside the home, in groups which, although superficially convivial and friendly, do not engage at more than a surface level with people's lives. Women's traditional relationship patterns of involvement with an extended family, neighbours and personal friends, do have more chance of some carry-over into daily life when help and support are needed; although the older person of either sex can find themself very alone and isolated, when people of their own age-group who have been lifelong friends are no longer there.

To maintain normal physical energy and health the two main requirements are suitable diet and the right amount of exercise. If you are thinking of going back to work or study after some time away from either, you need to realise that your physical, mental and nervous systems, and perhaps your emotional system as well, are going to be put under pressure greater than they have been used to for some time. This may well be permanent, as you move on from training and education into a full-time job. This in itself is no bad thing, as success in study and work will bring increased self-confidence and the rewards of income, interest and job-satisfaction as your career progresses, but you will have to adjust to surviving increased pressure most of the time, and to surviving unreasonable excess pressure on occasions.

## How can I achieve a balanced life?

We need now to go back to the idea of leading a balanced life, which we first looked at in Unit 1. It's something that everybody should aim to do all the time, whatever their life circumstances; but it's also something very difficult to achieve in practice, and many people find it almost impossible for quite long periods of their lives. Again, if you know what you want to aim for, there is a better chance of moving towards it than if you don't, and it's far easier to keep a sense of perspective when things are going wrong. Figure 15.1 shows a simplified presentation of the main areas of life in which we need to find a balance. Physical health and well-being, mental stimulation through work and leisure interests, and the social and emotional fulfilment of good relationships with family, friends and, hopefully, colleagues, all interact with each other, and the person with a balanced life has enough of all three. I have tried to place people with various different lifestyles on the diagram, in order to look at what changes they need to make.

The single person with a job or career they enjoy starts at A. If they live alone and have no domestic help they can readily become physically tired through having to manage things on two fronts, and they may not feel equal

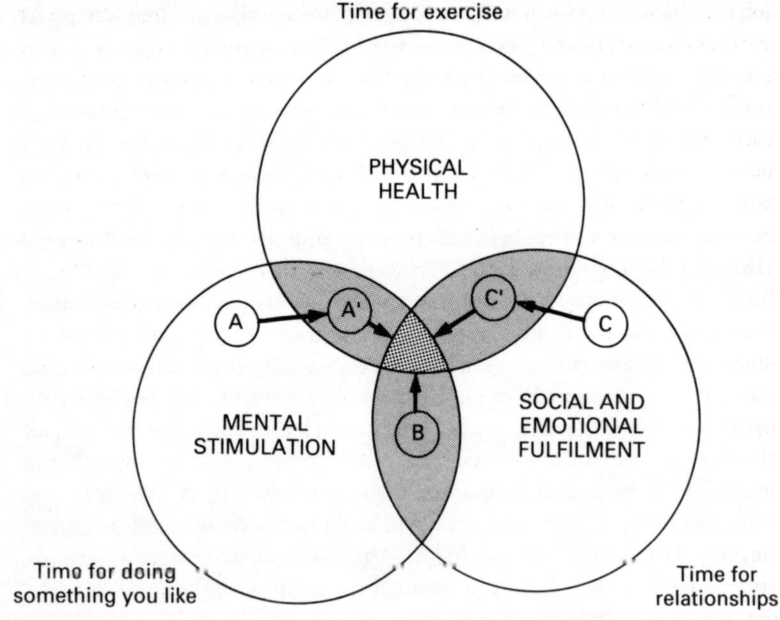


Figure 15.1 *Achieving a balance in life*

to making the physical effort to either go out and meet people or entertain friends at home. The situation can deteriorate until the person becomes so tired and lacking in the personal input from social life that they start to feel resentful of what their job takes from them and haven't enough energy to devote to leisure interests that are normally a source of stimulation. A person in this situation may have enough money to pay for domestic help, if they can organise themself to take advantage of it, and so move to A[1], where they have more energy to enjoy themself socially and can move towards the balance centre. The single person who lives with older parents may well find themself starting at A[1] and moving into the centre very easily, while the parents are in good health and reasonably energetic enough to deal with household responsibilities. They could, however, slip imperceptibly but irreversibly into a totally different kind of situation, as parents age and become infirm or handicapped, and the middle-aged single person finds themself in the role of sole carer, which leaves them in much the same situation as a single parent, but without knowing when their situation will be eased.

The family person with a job or career starts at B, assuming that they have job stimulation and the fulfilment of a good social and family life. When both partners in a relationship do paid work, there may be sufficient money for enough paid help to relieve both people of the heaviest burdens of domestic routine, and free their energies to spend leisure time more productively with each other and their family and friends, moving them from B towards the balance centre. If a family person tries to combine a demanding full-time job with single-handed running of a home and caring for children, they will become progressively more exhausted and unable to do any of these things as effectively as they would like. The answer for anyone who has too much to do for their own good is in delegation and sharing. If the person at home is over-loaded, partner and children need to take on more responsibility. If there is enough money for luxuries, some of these should be dispensed with and the money spent instead on paid domestic help. If the sole working person is over-loaded, over-worked, under stress or underpaid, the partner at home should start to think what they can do to relieve the situation, before breakdown or death does it for them.

The person living at home, with or without children, busy but with no financial need to work, may feel emotionally quite happy but lack the stimulation that the outside interest of a job gives. The person working outside the home in a job that requires a lot of shift work or overtime but is basically routine and unstimulating, can be happy in their family life but discontented otherwise. Both of these people are at risk of becoming physically very tired, through being on the job all the time, and ending up mentally under-stimulated because they have no time and energy for any interests of their own. They are the people at C in Figure 15.1, and they should try to organise their lives to get back first energy and then some mental stimulation, from a new job or some new hobbies, even some new friends, to move themselves eventually towards the balance centre.

## EXERCISES ON MONITORING YOUR HEALTH

**1. Over the course of a year, preferably over two to three years, check every day and record, in your diary or on a calendar, how you feel in the following ways:**

**WELL ........................................ UNWELL**
**ENERGETIC ............................ TIRED**
**UNSTRESSED ....................... STRESSED**
**OPTIMISTIC ......................... DEPRESSED**

You needn't write details; just a letter or mark you can identify for yourself. You could, if you wish, give yourself a daily score on a scale from 1 to 5, according to how good you feel on each count. The advantage of doing this on a calendar or year-planner is that you can see if there are times in the year when you are particularly susceptible to stress, depression, exhaustion or feeling below par, and can then try to identify recurring reasons for this. Winter and spring are particularly trying periods for physical health and morale, but these low periods should not last indefinitely.

Feeling persistently tired and unwell could indicate an underlying health problem that needs medical attention, or just poor diet and poor sleep. Feeling unrelievedly stressed and depressed could result from unresolved work and life problems that need to be faced and dealt with, or just insufficient relaxation and ineffective recreation. You can neither work nor study effectively

| Unit of competence 3: Managing stress | PERFORMANCE CRITERIA |
|---|---|
| | Maintain normal health and weight |
| | Feel fit and energetic |
| | Do not get overtired |
| | |
| | |
| | |

Figure 15.2 *Managing stress*

**if you are dogged by fatigue, ill-health and depression, and chronic stress only compounds the ill-effects of these.**

2. **In this section on keeping moving, the three components of managing time, managing stress and conserving energy interact on each other, and make the fourth one of managing crises possible to cope with. Using Figure 15.2 work out your own *elements of competence* that go to make up *unit of competence 3* in Figure 4.1 in Unit 4. Decide what your personal *performance criteria* would be and enter them on Figure 15.1. Think what you can do about those criteria that you are failing to meet and act on what you decide.**

## UNIT 16. Managing Crises

We can define a crisis as something unexpected, of a serious nature, if not unwelcome then at least presenting uncomfortable choices, happening suddenly, and requiring important decisions to be made quickly. I would like to extend this idea to take in much that can happen at an earlier stage, as poor advance planning and unrealistic expectations of ourselves and others can lead to things reaching crisis point before action is taken. There can be a failure to recognise that a crisis is developing, or a refusal to confront it until it is staring us in the face. Some crises can seem like total non-events, such as the protracted loss of motivation, enthusiasm and a feeling of commitment, and similar crises of confidence that can beset any student of any age over the duration of a long study course.

When we first recognise a crisis as imminent the immediate gut reaction is likely to be panic, if we have enough energy to generate panic; or collapse of morale and a sense of being totally unable to cope, if we feel over-tired or run-down in health. Fatigue, ill-health and the feeling of being alone with problems can cause us to over-react and perhaps make inappropriate decisions or take ill-advised action. The stresses that situations and other people impose on us can undermine our judgement and self-confidence. The stresses that we transmit to others around us can impair relationships and personal and family life, making the crisis situation worse to contain and deal with. The emphasis here will be on preparation and advance planning, as far as is possible, using the time, stress and energy management techniques of Units 13, 14 and 15, and the personal support network worked out and developed in Unit 8.

## What will be my basic crisis containment strategy?

Whether a crisis is a practical one, such as time or money, or an academic one, such as failure to meet course deadlines and objectives, your immediate action should be to get the best possible professional advice from the people who understand your situation. These will usually be your tutors and course organisers, but they may include the administrative and managerial staff of your study institution, and even your loan manager or sponsoring body if the problem is a financial one. Any decision you take about the future of your course is a decision about the future of your life, and before you take any drastic decision you should go back to Unit 1 and review your life objectives. You should ask yourself whether or not you would be prepared to rewrite these as a consequence of the decision you propose to take. If the answer is 'No', you need to think again about every possible alternative strategy you could use to contain the problem; even some you might not like to think of at first, such as saying 'No' to the demands people are making of you, however much they think they have the right to do it.

I want to suggest here that the people you look to for on-going moral support and maintenance of enthusiasm and motivation, throughout your study course and at crisis points, should be your fellow-students and the people in your personal support network, rather than your family and your tutors. Your tutors are extremely busy professional people, almost always harassed and under pressure, and they have many people like you to look after. Members of your family, with the best will in the world, are not objective about your problems; they largely see you as a means of solving their own. The basic move in dealing with crises is to take responsibility for yourself; to own and contain your own problems, and not feel that it is someone else's job to solve them for you. The clearer you make it that you are self-sufficient and not dependent as a person, the more willing other people will be to spare what little time and energy they have to give you what help they can. If you can face a crisis in a relaxed physical and mental state, there is some chance that you will be able to think clearly enough to plan what best to do, communicate clearly enough to whoever is involved what it is you want to do and want them to do, and to get together enough energy to carry on and do something about it. Successful negotiation of a crisis can itself be a confidence-building experience for you, and can impress other people with your maturity, balance and competence.

## What crises can I plan to avoid?

If you have done your homework on the financial planning side before the start of your course, you should be able to manage the financial resources you have over the duration of your course. The main problem for most people over a period of time is cash flow; having enough money coming in regularly to meet outgoings and bills as they come along. If you are being financed by a grant or a loan, you will get all the money in one go, or at least in large instalments. The problem then is to keep enough in reserve to meet your commitments over the duration of the grant or loan, or until the next instalment. You do need to do the sums before you start to spend, and not allow what looks like a lot of money to go to your head. You also need to keep accounts, in a notebook, in pen and ink, throughout your course; even better, throughout your life.

As a mature student, and perhaps an older person, you need to take very seriously the ideas about managing time, coping with stress and conserving energy which have been dealt with in Units 13, 14 and 15. If you have household and family commitments, your daily, weekly, termly and annual schedules will be formidably complex, and unless things are managed carefully you stand to end up exhausted and run-down in health, and dealing with neither home nor study commitments properly. You need to keep physically well, and mentally and nervously relaxed but energised, to stand the pace and meet the demands of a high-level academic course. Avoiding stress is an impossibility, and it probably wouldn't do us any good if we could. Most people respond to low level stress as stimulation and find it gets them mobile, when they might otherwise take things a bit too easy or put off starting things for a bit too long. Some people like quite a high level of stress when they are working towards deadlines or completing assignments, and find it makes them more effective and their work more enjoyable. It's the stress that you don't want that causes trouble, and one of the major factors contributing to its ill-effects is poor and ineffective use of leisure, in a life where fun, enjoyment and recreation are not given enough of their proper place. You need to get clear boundaries between what we called in Unit 13 *discretionary time* and *non-discretionary time*, and to apply them consistently.

## What crises are unpredictable?

Crises that cannot be predicted but will almost certainly happen include personal illness or the illness of a member of your family. This can be something minor that necessitates no more than a couple of days off, for yourself or to look after a sick child, or something that may have to be repeated regularly, if an older person you are caring for needs repeated attention over a longer period. If you know you are going to be absent, or suspect that you may have to be, inform the tutors concerned in advance and say that you will catch up with any work you have missed as soon as possible. Ask someone in your class or tutor group to take extra copies for you of any material given out. If you have made good friends with class colleagues, someone may be kind enough to let you photocopy their lecture notes. The important thing is to remember to return the compliment, should anyone else ever need your help.

There are some personal crises that everyone hopes will not happen to them, whether they are a student or not. One of these is the death of a close relative or friend, and unfortunately this is something that most of us have to face up to at some time or other. The physical arrangements that need to be made at the time of a death can be carried out very quickly. The mental, emotional and social readjustments that make up the process of bereavement can take much, much longer to run their course, and the experience of recovery is a very individual one, even if it goes normally. Should anything like this happen during your course, it would be wise to contact the student counselling services at your college or university, as there will almost certainly be times when you will need to talk to someone. If you are a distance-learning student and have no convenient access to student counselling services, your first point of contact will have to be with your personal tutor. The Open University incorporates provision for basic educational counselling into its system by assigning each student to a personal tutor/counsellor, part of whose role is to help the student to limit the damage that crises can have on their study programme and to give the student support and encouragement to continue working through difficult periods.

Another kind of crisis which most students experience at some time or other during their course is the loss of enthusiasm and motivation. Depression and slumps in interest are quite usual for a person doing a long course. It can feel like a crisis when the excitement you started out with just goes; perhaps for months on end. Fatigue, being below par in health, and social isolation are major contributors to this very debilitating state of mind and emotions. Times like the end of term, the approach to end-of-session and final exams, and the half-way point of the course as a whole, are when you can expect to feel low. When you are coming up to the half-way point with any long project, there will be times when you will wonder why you ever took it on. After the half-way point you will slowly begin to be aware of light at the end of the tunnel, and you will be able to work on out of an awareness of your own commitment to the course, whatever you feel like on a day-to-day basis.

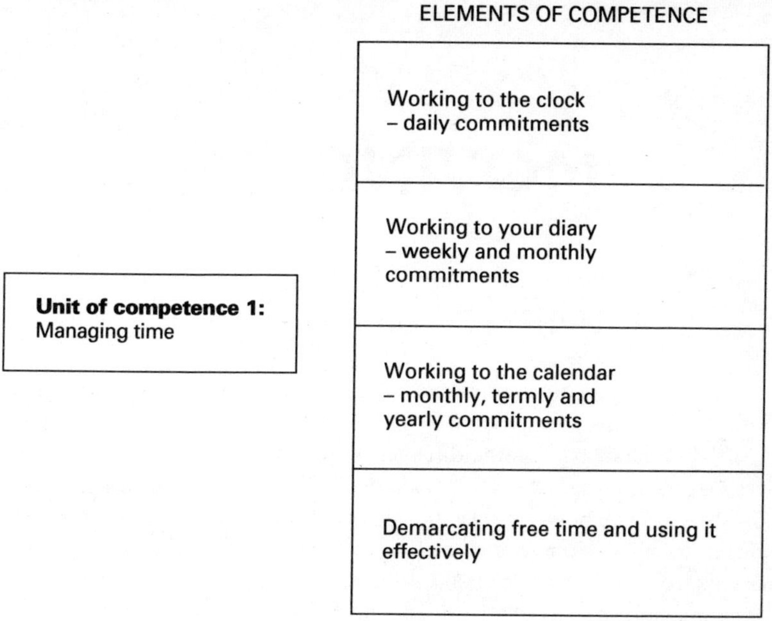

ELEMENTS OF COMPETENCE

| Unit of competence | Elements of competence |
|---|---|
| **Unit of competence 1:** Managing time | Working to the clock – daily commitments |
| | Working to your diary – weekly and monthly commitments |
| | Working to the calendar – monthly, termly and yearly commitments |
| | Demarcating free time and using it effectively |

Figure 16.1 *Managing time*

## EXERCISES ON AVOIDING PREDICTABLE PROBLEMS

**Using Figure 16.1 work out your own *performance criteria* for the *elements of competence* that go to make up *unit of competence 1* in Figure 4.1 of Unit 4. Do this in terms of appointments kept, routines completed, deadlines met and plans executed. Add your own criteria for demarcating free time for yourself, your relationships and your interests on a daily, weekly, termly and annual schedule.**

# V
# MOVING ON

## UNIT 17. Achieving Aims

If you've done your work properly in drawing up a calendar of major course and life events over the duration of your course, you will see that the academic year falls into six main parts: three terms and three blocks of holiday. They are meant to be used like this, and although you will have work assignments to do during your holidays, they should not take up all of your recreation time. If they are doing, either you are making too heavy weather of them, or you are being given too much work to do. Neither of these situations is unusual, but both are unreasonable, and you should decide, in consultation with your course colleagues if possible, what is happening and what can be done about it. Don't battle on with the impossible. Get support from your course colleagues and approach your senior tutor about it. If younger people can't cope with the workload, it's too much.

Older students tend to be extremely painstaking and conscientious about all aspects of their course work, whereas the younger student who has learned via the GCE 'A' level route from school that the important thing is to pass exams, and to pass them as well as possible, will concentrate maximum attention on doing just that, and may make only an average effort with course assignments that carry fewer marks. If you seem to be working harder than younger course colleagues, this might be what is happening, and you may need to take stock of what you really want from your course, and decide if you are being over-committed to parts of it that are going to be less productive of final marks than examinations will be. Younger students can be misleadingly casual all the way along the line and rivetingly committed when it comes to the count-down to final examinations. They focus their energies precisely where it matters, and refuse to exhaust themselves on peripheral things.

### How shall I ever make it?

You will have, from time to time, crises of morale and confidence that will undermine your belief in yourself and your will to succeed as a student. The longer your course goes on the greater number of these you can expect, and people undertaking study courses of up to 10 years length part-time should be aware of what their own powers of persistence are like, as dropping out at whatever stage is a loss of your time and energy investment to date. A negotiated withdrawal for a short intermission to your programme, preferably no longer than a year, is a different matter, but you should set yourself a deadline for return. Slumps in morale and enthusiasm take standard recurrent patterns; over a term, over a year, or over however many years your course lasts, and it helps to be prepared for them.

The beginning of a new course is marked by a high level of the four basics: motivation, confidence, commitment and enthusiasm. This gets you going and through about the first 40–50 per cent of the time commitment, say the first few weeks of a new term. If you are an energetic person and a careful time and energy manager, you may feel fine for longer than this. But some people do find that just around the halfway mark their energy starts to decline and that this can sap enthusiasm and confidence. Once past the halfway mark there is increasing light at the end of the tunnel and they can pick up and carry on. Probably everyone finds that the last 20–25 per cent of the time commitment, say the last two to three weeks of a term, leaves them drained and exhausted, particularly if there have been term or sessional exams to prepare for.

The loss of energy and enthusiasm that you can experience during the course of a term is repeated over the course of the academic year, with traditional slumps in morale at the end of the winter term, when illness over winter and the problems of bad weather can tend to leave people feeling depressed anyway. The summer term with its build-up to sessional examinations is always a time when one last big effort has to be made. If your course is a 3-year one, you may find that the middle year is the one you have to watch. Once into the final year you are nearly 70 per cent of the way there, and can see your objective as within reach. If you are studying part-time, look after yourself during the middle years particularly. Years 3 and 4 of a 5-year course, and the earlier years of a longer course, are the times when motivation can be lost. Before you yield to the temptation to give up, go back to Unit 1 and do your objective-setting again, and then forward to Unit 20 to see what's at the end of the road for you.

## Why haven't I done as well as I hoped?

This is a question that students of any age, and mature students in particular, can find themselves asking repeatedly, not just over individual assignments on a week-by-week basis, but finally over their whole course and its outcome. Everyone hopes for the best possible outcome for themself, but what people can fail to realise is that this is going to be different for different people. We do have different levels of basic intelligence, different intellectual abilities and different approaches to advanced study. This is saying nothing special; everyone is aware of it. It only becomes controversial when other people insist on deciding on our behalf what our differences and limitations are, without allowing us the right and opportunity to find out for ourselves.

It is a mistake for any mature student to think that older should mean wiser, and find themself completely thrown when teenagers in the same class get better marks. The wisdom that may, or may not, come to some of us with age is nothing to do with general intelligence, academic ability or study skills, though it can be a useful addition to this repertoire. Younger people in their late teens are adults, not children, and have the full adult range of intellectual abilities, perhaps at their most incisive. They lack only experience, of life and their subject, and they are quickly acquiring this. They have also been intellectually honed by the examination system to perform and compete, which may be something that the older student, eased and reassured into the system by the access route, has yet to learn; or decide against. The modern trend in assessment and examining is to allow the student to build up marks throughout their course by means of practical projects and written assignments. These can contribute up to 50 per cent of the final mark on which the award is based. If you feel you are reluctant to trust yourself to give your optimum performance in examinations, make extra sure that you do the continuous assessment components of your course as competently as you can, without expending excessive time and commitment on them.

It is also a misapprehension for any student to think that final awards are made for hard work and time commitment. They are made for performance, and in most courses this means final examination performance. Hard work and time commitment there has to be, but these alone are not enough, and it is wise as a student to make yourself aware how much of your final result depends on examination performance, and to make sure that you are capable of performing your best. The run-up to sessional and final examinations is a very exacting time, demanding peak effort and concentration directed on to the target of final papers. It is important to have managed time, energy, stress and crises well enough during the course to ensure that you are not burnt-out or too exhausted to make that final run and jump the last hurdle. With Units 13, 14, 15 and 16 behind you, you shouldn't be.

## What did I really want from this course anyway?

Most students have to accept disappointments at some stage or other of their study course. There will always be the assignment or essay that you worked hard on, but which wasn't quite what your tutor wanted. You may feel that you were utterly committed to attending lectures and tutorials, but that people who weren't have got on better in their examinations. That's up to them. They took a calculated risk and it paid off. One of the things you may have to accept as an older student is that you are less good at taking risks and may be better off playing safe and aiming for something you are reasonably confident of getting. Don't be disappointed in your final result, whatever it is. It's a major life achievement if you pass. And if you fail, it is hardly ever an irrecoverable failure, though it may well feel like it at the time.

Wherever you possibly can, try to regard failure to achieve what you wanted, and could reasonably have been expected to achieve, as some kind of learning experience rather than as an unmitigated disaster. If you have put in the necessary effort beforehand, you are very unlikely to fail final examinations, unless you are ill on the day or have had to cope with the stress of a serious personal crisis, such as bereavement. In cases like this, if you have built up a consistently good work record, your tutors are empowered to consider the possibility of allowing you a re-sit in whatever examination you have failed. It may even be unnecessary if you have a good enough performance on other papers. If a student is not really equal to the academic demands of the course they are on, it will be apparent quite early on, and tutors will usually advise a change of course or subject to something at which the student is much more likely to succeed.

### EXERCISES ON MONITORING ACHIEVEMENT

**In Exercise 1 of Unit 8 I asked you to draw up year-planners for your study, work and holiday schedules over the next three years. From what we have looked at in this unit, identify times, such as examinations, when you will need to feel physically, mentally and emotionally at your best, and also at your most alert, relaxed and focused in concentration. Good stress management techniques, such as mentioned in Unit 14, should help with this. Identify also times when you can predictably expect to feel less than your best, such as at the end of winter and towards the end of terms and sessions. As you do the exercises set at the end of Unit 15, make**

**comparisons between your own ups-and-downs in health, well-being and morale and the demands that will be made on you by your course schedule. Look carefully for any places where peak performance will be expected of you at times when you can expect to feel less than your best, and look after yourself extra carefully before, during and after these times.**

## UNIT 18. Accepting Change

The peak experience of an academic study course is usually after the last examination, when most students are aware that, give or take a few marks, they are through. This is the time when younger people will go out and celebrate together, both their shared achievements and their shared friendships, soon to come to an end as they move out into the external world of work and wage-earning. Such celebrations mark the onset of a major life transition and are an informal acknowledgement of separation from academic life and studenthood. The formal incorporation into the adult life of being a graduate comes on graduation day, when students' parents, spouses and families or friends are invited to attend the formal award-giving ceremony and share the official recognition of the student's academic achievement. If you are a part-time student there will still be a sense of shared participation and closeness as you reach the end of your time together. You should try to arrange to get together after your last exam, and again later, maybe when your results come through.

If you have done your course by distance-learning or flexi-study you may well not know who your course colleagues are, unless your institution has made arrangements to give you the opportunity to contact each other or meet. This is a sad loss, but it is inevitable when you have to undertake your advanced study by one of these methods. If you are with the Open University, you may have made friends through tutorials and summer schools, so do, if you can, celebrate your achievements together. It is very important to involve your family in the actual award-giving ceremony, as few people have actually attended a graduation day, and when they do they find the whole event deeply impressive and moving. It is your way of showing your family what you have achieved academically and how it is being formally recognised by the academic establishment, and your way of giving them your thanks and a share in the final outcome.

## How shall I feel when it's all over?

The peak experience of knowing you've made it as you complete your final exams is followed quite soon by the culmination of the course in your official graduation day. You will probably stay on a mental and emotional high during the whole of this time and for perhaps a few weeks afterwards. After that you will slowly come to realise that your course has finally ended, your course colleagues have dispersed, and that within a few weeks your places in the classrooms and lecture theatres will be occupied by other students about to embark on their own higher education studies. Good as your relationships with your tutors and other staff of the institution have been, they are now at an end. One thing you can do before you finally part is to make a point of saying goodbye and thanking all these people for their contribution to your achievement.

Probably the first negative emotion you will have to deal with is a sense of anti-climax. Your highly developed confidence and sense of commitment have no longer any immediate object. Your enthusiasm and motivation no longer have a clear sense of direction. This is the neutral region of a life transition, when everything goes into a state of flux between the separation from one way of life and the incorporation into another. Whatever your life style and life conditions you will need to gather together the valuable skills and resources you have developed over the years of your course and channel them into something new. Enthusiasm and motivation have to have a purpose, and without an object, confidence and commitment will gradually fade away. You will need to find a new focus for your mental energy and a place in your life for your new skills and interests. Before you start seriously to re-plan your life, take a break, not just from study but from everything.

## What will success do for my self-image?

Your self-esteem and self-confidence will be at an all-time high as you graduate, and you will probably feel a greater sense of self-worth and achievement than you ever have before, particularly if you are a person who for many years believed that higher education was not really for you. That you were sold this idea originally by a misguided society, perhaps at a time when there was no financial assistance available to even very deserving prospective students from anything less than affluent backgrounds, was a grave miscarriage of social justice, but the society of the post-war years has done its best to compensate for what was lacking previously, and you can congratulate yourself that, through your own effort and determination, you have finally managed to arrive at where you should be on the educational pyramid; maybe not at the top, but at least somewhere on the structure.

It is important for you to consolidate the impetus of your achievement before you start on what should be a continuous upward movement and development throughout the rest of your life, as this can, if the impetus is not taken, be the beginning of slipping away from a summit of achievement back into the academic mediocrity it took you so much effort to emerge from. This is less of a problem for the younger person, whose newly-acquired qualification will almost certainly, sooner or later, get them into a job. For the older graduate, who is already in a job, this is the time to advise your employer of your enhanced qualifications, and to ask what scope and prospects there are for you now that you are a different calibre of professional person. If there are none, you would be wise to take careers advice, and either look elsewhere or undertake career restructuring, unless you are content to stay where you are for the foreseeable future.

What you know, what you can do and what you are interested in doing are major features of the personality you present to other people, and now that, for you, these things have changed beyond recognition, you must make it apparent by external changes in your life that show the internal changes are here to stay. You will be helped in Unit 19 to present yourself to the world of employment by writing your new achievements into your cv, and you will be given the chance in Unit 20 to think about and state your renewed life and work aims. Even if you have no immediate need to work and have just undertaken advanced study for your own satisfaction, don't spend too long just sitting back on your laurels congratulating yourself on having got a degree. Young people can't; they have to get out into the world of work and get on with life, if only to repay their student loans. Among the most boring people in middle-age are those who got a degree years ago, have never done anything since, and have no on-going interest in their own subject.

## Will other people realise I have changed?

The major part of educational change is in inward mental, cultural and emotional growth, and how much of this will be relayed to other people in your relationships and social interactions with them will depend on who these people are and how sensitive they are to the changes in you. If you wish to be accepted by other people as a changed person, you need to show evidence of what change there has been. You do, in fact, have to be prepared to prove that you are different. This may take the form of restructuring your career to take on something which demands the qualifications you now have and which you couldn't have done before. Or it may be that you can seek promotion in your present job, or move into an area of greater work responsibility and interest that your employer might not have entrusted you with before you graduated. The thing that you need to do in your private life is to take up new interests that are commensurate with your intellectual abilities, and to make the kind of friends who share those interests and the sense of values you have developed about them and about the other ways in which you spend your life.

It would be a useful exercise here to look back over your personal contact network and see how it has grown and developed during your time as a higher education student. You need at this stage to review it and to make some strong decisions about who stays on it and why and, perhaps more importantly, who goes. There may be long-standing friends with whom you have shared a lot of activities in the past and with whom you may be reluctant to part, but if they are unable to appreciate who you are as you are now there will be little future in your relationship with them. You will not have the time for unrewarding relationships of limited understanding. What you need for the future are the kind of people who will give you the kind of positive affirmation that is a source of strength in life and who will reinforce your belief in yourself.

You need to be aware of what you need from people, and we shall spend some time at the end of this unit thinking about how to decide that, and about how to decide who is giving you what you need and who isn't any longer. Your personal contact network is the area of life where you have more choice. Certain family relationships, on your own and on your partner's side may be near-unchangeable, and not worth wasting energy doing any more than tolerate.

## EXERCISES ON NETWORK MAINTENANCE

**1. Who needs to be told that you now have a degree?**

**Think of your employer and work colleagues, your community and group interest contacts, your neighbours, relatives and friends. Don't be surprised or upset if some of them do not fully share your joy and are a little slow to tender their congratulations. Many people envy an achievement but would not envy the work that goes into getting it. Tell them anyway.**

**2. From the personal contact network you drew up in Exercise 2 of Unit 8 decide who you would like to take onwards with you into**

**your future life. There will have been an opportunity to find out during your course whose friendship is a source of moral support and affirmation to you, and who the people are who persist in seeing you as they always have done and are oblivious to changes in your life and personality.**

**This is an exercise in carrying over and carrying forward and I want to ask you to be quite ruthless in your assessments of what the relationships you have are giving you and doing for you. Go through everyone on your personal contact network, except the people you have already decided to drop from it, and answer the following 5 questions about them, scoring on a scale of 1 to 5 or 1 to 10 if you wish:**

**a. How far does this person relate to me as the person I am?**
**b. How far do they meet my needs?**
**c. How important to me is what we share?**
**d. How important to me will what we share be in 15 or 20 years' time?**
**e. How much development has there been in our relationship over the past 10 years?**

**These questions are quite probing and need a measure of self-awareness to answer. I'd also like to add that, however promising a relationship looks, if you are doing more than 50 per cent of the work of keeping it going, you are giving more than you get and should reconsider if you want to continue.**

**3. I'd like to suggest a list of 10 basic needs that most people try to have met in one way or another:**

| | |
|---|---|
| **spiritual** | **educational** |
| **practical** | **social** |
| **recreational** | **sexual** |
| **professional** | **emotional** |
| **intellectual** | **cultural** |

**Spiritual needs are concerned with your inner self-development as an integrated person; practical needs with getting through the routines of daily life; recreational needs with hobbies and leisure; professional needs with shared work and career interests; intellectual needs with shared ideas; and educational needs with being an informed and mentally developing person. It isn't necessary for these to be 10 basic needs for everybody. You can**

**drop some of mine and add your own instead. I'm using 10 as a convenient number in scoring exercises because you can get a final total out of 100 and have it as a readily assessable percentage figure. One hundred per cent is the most you could ever get or hope for; 75 per cent is three-quarters of the way there and perhaps the most you could reasonably expect of anybody; 50 per cent is half-way there and is the point at which you start to ask yourself questions about how much give-and-take is going on; 25 per cent is only a quarter of the maximum and it means that you are not getting the other three-quarters but giving it.**

**Choose about 20 people from your personal contact network and give them a mark out of 10 for what they contribute to meeting each of your 10 basic needs. Total their scores and compare them on a 25, 50, 75 and 100 per cent scale. Try to get at least 10 people who exceed 65 per cent. Whoever falls below 40 per cent, let them lapse from your network, unless what they contribute is very important indeed.**

# UNIT 19. Managing Outcomes

The real outcomes of a higher education study course are the changes in your personality, which then necessitate changes in your life aims, concerning both work *and* the people you work for and spend your leisure time with. None of these changes are instantly achievable, and you will need to think about and plan carefully how you tackle changes on the personal and job fronts. The benefits to your family relationships will be your enhanced earning prospects, whether you are in work now or about to take up work, and the fact that you are a happier and more fulfilled person who has gained by working themself into an expanded personal and professional role. It may take your family and friends some time to fully realise this, but you should persist, quietly but firmly, with building your new image and gradually you will come to be seen in the new perspective that you want.

## Where do I want to go from here?

Whatever age of student you are, you are now on the threshold of something different. Your life will never seem the same again to you, whatever other people think, and you are in probably your best-ever position to make some of the changes that you want. I am writing this in the middle of the longest recession we have experienced in the UK for decades, so I don't want to be falsely optimistic about things being achievable quickly. But I do want to emphasise that you are in the best position you could possibly be to do something with what there is going, and that you may never personally feel any stronger or better equipped to tackle problems. As you progress through life you will gain in experience, but it's doubtful if your energy, drive and enthusiasm will ever be higher than they are now.

If you are a younger mature student, say under 35, you have ahead of you up to 40 years of working life, and you will want this to be in jobs that will bring enough money for the life style you want to achieve. You also need to accept that you may not go straight up the same ladder all the time. You may have to change direction and move on to one or more different ladders, as work prospects in one area of employment contract with changing economic circumstances, and renewed prospects open up in other areas. The ideas of Unit 3 about acquiring accreditable competences are important here, as they form the basis of your repertoire of transferable skills that you can carry from one job to another. They need to be worked on and worked up as you go along, so that , as far as possible, your career changes are planned ahead, rather than precipitated as unpredictable crises that may force a change of direction that you do not want but have no control over.

If you are a middle of the age-range mature student, say 35 to 55, the chances are that you have returned to study because you are without a job and want one. You may be a woman who has taken a longish career break to bring up a family but who now wants to return to work. Perhaps at the time you withdrew from the labour market getting back was not particularly difficult for a woman professional, but you now find that avenues of employment have closed down and that new openings are few. You may be a woman who married and had a family early in life, without thinking that far ahead and now find that, as your children grow up and leave home, your role is running out before you have thought your way through to the next stage. You may be anyone, man or woman, who through early retirement or redundancy finds themself without a job before they want to be. If so, your main reason for returning to study may be to re-train and re-qualify in a new work area that offers a more promising future.

If you are an older mature student, say 55 plus, you may possibly, but only possibly, not need to worry about work or money, and may just have been free to undertake advanced study for your own self-development and fulfilment. You may have loved having an opportunity that should have been yours 40, 50 or 60 years ago, had society been as egalitarian as it is now. If you are this kind of person, you will not have needed my previous pep talk on maintaining your new self-image and keeping an on-going interest in your subject. You will value what you have acquired so much that letting it slip away is the last thing you would do. There is also the possibility that, as an early-retired person, you may need to look at work prospects to supplement your pension; or that, as a fully retired person, you may choose to invest some of your time in one of the many worthwhile kinds of voluntary work, for which your new professional skills could render you eminently suitable.

There will be a few readers who will want to go on to do some further study, either because they need it for the career they want or because their tutors think they are particularly promising students who could progress even further. If you have completed the basic Open University first degree (BA) or the basic part-time external BA through a university, polytechnic or college, you can enhance the class of your degree to honours level by adding extra credits over 2 or 3 years. You could also take a post-graduate master's degree (MA, MEd or MSc, for example) by research alone, or as a specialised advanced study course with a research component, either full-time as an internal student if you can get funding, or part-time at your own expense, often with one of the convenient modular arrangements, allowing for progress at your own pace within limits and accommodating intermission periods if needed. A course such as the Post Graduate Certificate in Education, for prospective graduate teachers, attracts a mandatory LEA grant. The career development loans mentioned in Unit 4 are another possible source of funding. Some students even go on to do a part-time doctoral degree (PhD) and end up being employed by the university that awarded it.

## How can I get to where I want to go?

Whatever age student you are, while you are still on roll as a student at your higher education institution, take advantage of whatever careers services the institution offers, and have the benefit of the advice and guidance of a professional careers officer, whether it is career launch, career progression or career restructuring that you want. You are also entitled to have an interview at your local Careers Office in your town or city of residence, and it is a good idea to ask to see an officer with experience in adult careers guidance.

If you are in a situation of not really knowing what you want to do, or if your previous job or career has folded and you need a total rethink, I should like to recommend that you do some self-help work on your own, as well as taking advantage of what is officially on offer. Those readers who are Open University students may already have seen the OU set book *Build your own Rainbow: A Workbook for Career and Life Management*. Amongst a wide range of other things, the authors deal in detail with the analysis of transferable skills. Starting from the point of finding out whether you are good at dealing with people, things, data or ideas, they move you towards being able to decide whether your main skills areas are practical, investigative, organisational, administrative, enterprising, social or artistic, and then on to what work areas would best match your best skills. For readers who need to make middle-life changes, financial and personal, a comparable approach is taken in *Changing Course: A Positive Approach to a New Job or Lifestyle.* Details of both books, and some others that you could find helpful, are given at the end of this book.

You should maintain a personal cv (curriculum vitae) showing details of your qualifications and work experience throughout life, including membership of professional associations and details of your academic and research interests and of any work you have had published. As you move on in your career you will need to constantly update your cv, and as you acquire more to add to it some of the older, less relevant things can be dropped. It is debatable how far you need to include personal things, such as sporting, recreational and cultural hobbies and interests. I think it is advisable to keep things down to the amount that can be word-processed on to one A4 sheet, with enough spacing for clear legibility. Whether or not there is room for much else will probably depend on how much career-oriented information you want to include. Some employers have their own application form, but as this will be a general one, a personal cv can always help to enlarge on and clarify certain points.

The standard cv format for presentation to most British employers is the chronological order one, starting from secondary school and progressing onwards through whatever you have done workwise or educationally to wherever you are now. As well as your personal education and work history, what a prospective employer will be looking for is unexplained gaps. If you have taken a career break to have a family, it makes a good impression if you can put forward activities such as voluntary work you have been involved in, to show that your organisational and work skills have been in current use during the break. Some employers, overseas rather than in UK, who do not understand the flexibility and quality of the UK higher education system, can fail to give sufficient regard to degrees obtained outside a higher education institution, so it might sometimes be a good idea just to state your degree and the awarding university. On the other hand, many UK employers take a special look at the applicant from a non-conventional background, feeling that if they started at an educational disadvantage then the person must have great drive and initiative to have got to where they are now.

**EXERCISES ON PROFESSIONAL COMPETENCES**

**From Figure 4.1 of Unit 4 we have left over *units of competence 9 and 10*, which are concerned with subject competence and research skills. I'd like to ask you to spend some time, quite a long time, breaking both of these down into *elements of competence*, or what you can do, and *performance criteria*, or when and where you have done it. Most of this will be subject-specific, though there will be some overlap on research skills. Make out your own subject competence analysis chart on a large sheet of paper. A preliminary brainstorming session, much as you did when you drew up a draft personal contact network in Exercise 3 of Unit 8, will bring your ideas out and you can then group them into *elements of competence* and decide what your *performance criteria* should be. It's advisable to let your mind work this over, in its quiet background way, taking perhaps two to three weeks, or even longer.**

**What I'm asking you to do here is to upgrade what we called *student competences* in Figure 4.1 of Unit 4 into your *professional competences*, which will form your repertoire of marketable skills as you approach the world of employment. In doing this you will be operating at, or above, NVQ Level 4 identified in Unit 3, in an area not yet fully worked out for more than a few professions. Your *elements of competence* will be the key skills that you emphasise on a skills-oriented cv and your *performance criteria* will be the supporting evidence that you have them, and will be what a traditional chronological cv will ask you to present as evidence when you make a job application. At the end of this exercise you will have the foundation of a personal job skills database, which you should compile carefully and efficiently on to a manual index or, better still, into computer store if you have one.**

# UNIT 20. Moving On

As we move into the last unit of this book I want to go back to reviewing some of the ideas first put forward in Unit 1 and to ask you to reconsider how far you have advanced towards incorporating them into your life. The idea of careership is crucial, particularly to the younger person, who will benefit most from starting out in adult working life with clear plans about their long-term life aims, and clear ideas about the intermediate work and life objectives they need to attain in order to achieve these aims. The components of careership are good objective-setting, careful recording of achievements, detailed analysis of competences acquired and transferable skills accumulated, and flexibility in matching your skills to the work prospects available. You must maintain regular review and a constant broad overview of your progress so that when a change in direction is needed you can anticipate and plan it, and pass through it like a surface ripple on life, rather than sink into unmanageable crisis and lose direction.

I also think that you should give your personal life as much attention as your career, and that whatever careership planning you are doing, it should be accompanied by personal life planning, incorporating the things you plan to do with your spouse or partner, family and friends, your personal network contacts; and for yourself, your own hobbies and interests. Personal and professional life support each other, and although there are times when one or other temporarily takes priority, such as when a career is building up or when someone leaves full-time work to have a family, the long-term aim should be balance, and having to accept too much of one at the expense of the other leaves life depleted and its quality impoverished.

## What style and quality of life do I want?

Going back to the idea of taking charge of your own career development, there is much available in terms of personal and professional self-development training for women, but nothing like enough for men. Women as members of the national workforce have been disadvantaged in the past and very strong moves are being made to redress the balance. Men on the whole have been expected to get their chance of grooming for advancement by looking promising to their immediate bosses and being moved into line for promotion as it becomes available. This has been all very well for men who fitted their senior colleagues' image of the establishment man, but it has done no service to able and enterprising men whose talents have not been recognised by the blinkered vision of over-confident and complacent power figures in a male hierarchical system. Women have taken up the challenge of their long disadvantage and there are many men who would benefit from taking up the kind of career development training that so many women now do.

The lesson that women have learned from men is that a career can benefit enormously from the right kind of guidance at the right time and from having its possibilities recognised by someone experienced enough to see objectively in the person what they lack the experience and detachment to see for themselves. Such a person can take on the role of mentor to someone younger whose career is still in the making, and their advice and insight can be invaluable. Successful men have always done this for up-and-coming younger men, and women's business and professional organisations are now moving to establish mentoring systems to help promising younger women move up the career ladder. The mentors are usually senior women, where they can be found, but not necessarily, and some senior men, to their credit, have started to see women's potential where it has always existed and to give them the guidance and opportunities needed to give a promising career a good start. What I would like to suggest here is that women, and men, should choose their own mentors, cultivate them socially and professionally, and establish a relationship in which they can access the mentor as needed. Mentors will not always choose us, and if we feel we are going unrecognised we need to find our own.

Throughout your career you will need to be constantly aware of the need for updating your existing skills and adding new ones to your repertoire. Take every opportunity your employer offers for training and diversification, and if they offer none, sort out something for yourself to do via the Open University, National Extension College or comparable institution, and ask for your employer's help with fees and expenses and possibly some limited time off. Your employer will benefit through your development as a worker, and you will be giving to and taking something from the system of which you are part. What you really need to be doing in your career is to be both working and planning ahead at the same time. The development of your career should be accompanied by the continuing enhancement of your professional skills and by the on-going development of your personal educational interests. Many people do both through associate studentship of the Open University, which offers the widest range of professional-level continuing education courses in the country.

## What difference will it all make to my life?

Perhaps the major difference that acquiring a higher education qualification will make to your life is that you will now know what things in life you want more time for, and you should ultimately be in a better position to earn enough money to make that possible. You will have acquired renewed expectations and higher aspirations; you will not be content to let other people decide what you should have and do; you will want to decide for yourself what and how much. You will have moved into Levels 3, 4 and 5 of the Maslow hierarchy of Unit 1, and the massive personal growth and self-development that you have undergone will have emerged into the self-realisation and self-awareness that accompanies the major life transition that high-level academic attainment is. You will also have acquired intellectual skills and mental discipline that will always be unmistakeably apparent to sensitive and discerning people who are on the same wavelength.

Because you have changed as a person, it is inevitable that the balance and dynamics of your closest relationships will need some re-adjustment. While one half of a couple is engaged in an advanced study course, which seems to alternate between an experience of a lifetime that the other half cannot share and a total withdrawal from mundane domestic matters into academic seclusion, the person left to keep the home fires burning and the family budget balanced can feel excluded and resentful. They can envy the opportunity that at this point is not theirs. It is far better to openly acknowledge these negative feelings so that something can be done about them, if not now then later. Whoever accepts both the freedom and constraint of being able to commit themself to their own self-development over the duration of an advanced study course should, in their turn, be willing to do what is necessary to make it possible for their other half to do the same when he or she wishes.

For some couples, the temporary drawing-apart that the total absorption of one partner in study makes inevitable, foreshadows gently the drawing-apart that many couples experience in middle age as children grow up and leave home. There is a personal separateness that we have to develop as individual people in the course of our lives, and this can be suppressed or displaced in the demanding years when children are being brought up. The sense of separateness as individuals can strike both partners quite sharply when the cementing pressures of family life are released; and it requires both renewal and readjustment to get back to the unity of purpose and diversity of individual personality that a mature relationship requires. If you have dealt with this situation once in life, it will not prove a problem later on. Certainly, nothing as impermanent as just attending a study course need shake a relationship apart, unless that relationship is on shaky ground already. It is the outcome of the educational process that has to be accepted, cannot be denied and must be taken account of, in all subsequent relationship renewals. On this tentatively serious but not unoptimistic note I'd like to leave you. So, thank you for reading, thank you for thinking about what you've been reading, and good luck for the future in life, work, study, or whatever else you get involved in in the pursuit of your happiness.

## EXERCISES ON DECISION-MAKING

**Go back to the exercises on motivation at the end of Unit 1 and review what changes you would like to make in view of your own personal and professional development and enhanced qualifications. You can repeat the objective-setting exercises of Unit 1 as they stand, or alternatively just set up a table of short, medium and long-term objectives based on Figure 20, placing the personal alongside the professional and including anything that you want to include from the balanced life wheel in Figure 1.2. Review these objectives at intervals in your own short, medium and long-term future. Good luck with them!**

| | | Major objectives | Earliest date for achievement | Review of progress |
|---|---|---|---|---|
| Professional and career | 1 | | | |
| | 2 | | | |
| | 3 | | | |
| | 4 | | | |
| | 5 | | | |
| Personal and social | 1 | | | |
| | 2 | | | |
| | 3 | | | |
| | 4 | | | |
| | 5 | | | |

Figure 20.1 *Setting personal and professional objectives*

# ADDITIONAL READING

## Study Skills

*How to Win as a Part-time Student*, Tom Bourner and Phil Race, Kogan Page, 1990.

*Returning to Study*, Christopher Beddows, Heinemann Educational, 1989.

*Adult Study Tactics: A Springboard to Learning*, Di Percy, Macmillan, 1989.

*The Good Study Guide*, Andrew Northedge, Open University, 1990.

*Academic Writing Course*, RR Jordan, Collins ELT, 1990.

*Sounds to Reason: A Guide to Argument Assessment*, GM Hibbins, Macmillan, 1980.

*Studying for Science*, Brian White, E & FN Spon, 1991.

*Scientists must Write*, Robert Barrass, Chapman & Hall, 1978.

*Starting Statistics*, EL Hanson and GA Brown, Hulton, 1969.

*English in Context*, Patricia McEldowney, Nelson, 1982.

*Women Working it Out*, Dr Jane Chapman, COIC, Moorfoot, Sheffield S1 4PQ, 1989/90.

*Returning to Work*, The Women Returners' Network, Kogan Page, 1992.

*How to Get a Job after 45, The Daily Telegraph Guide*, Julie Bayley, Kogan Page, 1990.

There are many excellent books on study skills and these few will give you a start if you want to move on into higher education. If you are interested in developing the kind of holistic thinking described in Unit 10, Tony Buzan's books are very popular and easy to read. If you feel you need extra help with English grammar and the basic skills of listening, speaking, reading and writing, can I suggest that you look at the range of books on sale for English as a Foreign Language. These are used by state and private language schools, in the UK and throughout the world, to train overseas professional people who want to study English to enter higher education in an English-speaking country, or to improve their professional qualifications and career prospects in their own countries. Longman, Collins, Penguin, Oxford and Cambridge, amongst other publishers, produce a quality range of books and tapes. You can get publishers' addresses from the *Writers' and Artists' Yearbook* in the public library, send for catalogues and make your own choice. Bournemouth English Book Centre (Freefone 0800 262260) can help with supplying orders quickly if you have any local difficulty. You should be looking at intermediate and advanced levels for your study purposes.

## Career Planning

*How to Write a CV*, University of London Careers Advice Service, 50 Gordon Square, London WC1H 0PQ.
*How to Write a Winning CV*, Alan Jones, Hutchinson, 1990.
*Preparing your own CV*, Rebecca Corfield, Kogan Page, 1990.
*How to Face the Interview*, Clive Fletcher, Unwin Paperbacks, 1986.
*Successful Interview Skills*, Rebecca Corfield, Kogan Page, 1992.
*How to Get that Job*, Rebecca Corfield, Kogan Page, 1992.
*Applying for a Job in English*, MD Spooner and JS McKellen, Penguin, 1990.
*How to Manage your own Career*, Ben Ball, British Psychological Society and Kogan Page, 1989.
*Managing your own Career*, Dave Francis, Fontana Collins, 1985.
*Networking and Mentoring*, Dr Lily Segerman-Peck, Judy Piatkus, 1991.
*What Colour is your Parachute? A Manual for Job Hunters and Career Changers*, Richard Nelson Bolles, Ten Speed Press, 1987.
*Build your own Rainbow: A Workbook for Career and Life Management*, Barrie Hopson and Mike Scally, Lifeskills Communications, Mercury Books, 1992.
*Changing Course: A Positive Approach to a New Job or Lifestyle*, Maggie Smith, Mercury Books, 1992.
*Going Freelance*, Godfrey Golzen, Kogan Page, 1989.

## Managing Time and Stress

*How to Get Control of your Time and your Life*, Alan Laikein, Signet, 1973.
*The Joy of Stress*, Dr Peter Hanson, Pan, 1986.
*Stress and Relaxation*, Jane Madders, Martin Dunitz, 1979.
*The Transcendental Meditation Technique*, Peter Russell, Routledge and Kegan Paul, 1977.
*Stress Check* (and other more recent books by Cary Cooper on stress management), Cary Cooper, Prentice Hall, 1981.

*Don't Say Yes when you want to Say No*, Herbert Fensterheim and Jean Baer, Futura, 1976.
*When I say No I feel Guilty*, Manuel J Smith, Bantam, 1975.
*Your Erroneous Zones*, Wayne Dyer, Sphere, 1979.
*Pulling your own Strings*, Wayne Dyer, Hamlyn, 1978.
*A Woman in your own Right*, Anne Dickson, Quartet Books, 1982.

## References

*Motivation and Personality*, Abraham Maslow, Harper and Row, 1970.
*Passages: Predictable Crises of Adult Life*, Gail Sheehy, Corgi/Bantam, 1977.
*Pathfinders*, Gail Sheehy, Sidgwick & Jackson, 1983.
*The Seasons of a Man's Life*, DJ Levinson, CN Darrow, EB Klein, MH Levinson and B McKee, Alfred Knopf, 1978.
*Taking Stock: Being 50 in the 80s*, Charles Handy, BBC Publications, 1983.
*Transition: Understanding and Managing Personal Change*, John Adams, John Hayes and Barrie Hopson, Martin Robertson, 1976.

# USEFUL INFORMATION

## Reference books on higher education entrance (available in public libraries, and mostly updated annually)

*University Entrance: The Official Guide 1992*, compiled by the Committee of Vice-Chancellors and Principals of UK Universities.

*The Complete Degree Course Offers*, Brian Heap, Trotman and Co Ltd.

*Directory of First Degree and Diploma in Higher Education Courses*, Council for National Academic Awards (CNAA).

*Your Choice at 17+* (Degree and all HE courses) Careers Research and Advisory Council (CRAC), Hobson's Press.

*University Entrance: Mature Students Going to University; A Parents' Guide*, University Central Council for Admissions (UCCA). (Free: send A5 envelope.)

*Polytechnic Courses Handbook*, compiled by the Committee of Directors of Polytechnics.

*A Survey of Polytechnic Courses*, Eric Whittington, Trotman and Co Ltd.

*A Compendium of Advanced Courses in Colleges of Further and Higher Education: Full-time and Sandwich Courses in Polytechnics and Colleges outside the University Sector*, London & SE Regional Advisory Council for Education and Training.

*Colleges and Institutes of Higher Education Guide*, compiled by the Standing Conference of Principals. Free guide and leaflet from The Administrative Officer, Standing Committee of Principals (SCP), Edge Hill College of Higher Education, Ormskirk, Lancs L39 4QP.

*Part-time Degrees, Diplomas and Certificates: A Guide to Part-time Higher Education Courses at Universities, Polytechnics and Colleges*, Malcolm Tight, Careers Research and Advisory Council (CRAC), Hobson's Press.

*Scottish Central Institutions Handbook*, compiled by Paisley College of Technology on behalf of SCI.

*Directory of Technical and Further Education*, Longman.

*Kogan Page Mature Student's Handbook*, Margaret Korving, Kogan Page Ltd.

*The Open Learning Directory 1992*, (Pergamon Open Learning).

The majority of these reference books are annually updated by the bodies responsible for producing them, and you should consult a good public library for current editions. As the UK Higher Education system is currently under review, institutions are undergoing processes of restructure and regrading, and many will probably be renamed within the next two to three years. Polytechnics are likely to be designated as universities and many higher education colleges as university colleges. The attributions and information given here are correct at the time of going to press, but the reader needs to be aware of forthcoming changes and to make the adjustment in reading when these are implemented.

## Financial information for prospective students

| | |
|---|---|
| **DES** | *Student Grants and Loans: A Brief Guide 1991–92*<br>Published by the Department of Eduation and Science (DES), DES Publications Dispatch Centre, Honeypot Lane, Stanmore, Middlesex HA7 1AZ. |
| **LEA** | Also obtainable from your Local Education Authority (LEA); Contains information for students in Scotland and Northern Ireland as well as England and Wales. |
| **EGAS** | Education Grants Advisory Service<br>Information about non-statutory sources of funding, with particular reference to educational trusts; advice given about statutory help if appropriate. The Student Adviser, EGAS, Family Welfare Association, 501–505 Kingsland Road, London E8 4AU. |
| **DE/COIC** | *Sponsorships 1992*<br>Lists employers and professional bodies offering sponsorship for first degrees, BTEC higher awards and comparable courses. Contact Department CW, ISCO5, The Paddock, Frizinghall, Bradford BD9 4HD. (Department of Employment and COIC) |
| **SED** | *Guide to Students' Allowances (Scotland)*<br>Scottish Education Department Awards Branch, Haymarket House, Clifton Terrace, Edinburgh EG12 5DT. |
| **PCAS** | Industrial Sponsorship and PCAS<br>Information from PCAS. |

**SLC** Student Loans Company Limited
100 Bothwell Street, Glasgow G2 7JD

**Reference books** *The Grant Register* (Macmillan Press); *Directory of Grant-making Trusts* (Charities Aid Foundation).

## Useful addresses for prospective students

**UCCA** University Central Council for Admissions
PO Box 28, Cheltenham, Gloucester GL50 3SA.

**PCAS** Polytechnic Central Admissions System
PO Box 67, Cheltenham, Gloucester GL50 3AP.

**CRCH** Central Register and Clearing House
3 Crawford Place, London W1H 2BN.

**OU** The Open University, Central Enquiry Service, PO Box 71, Milton Keynes MK7 6AG.

**OU** The Open University, Undergraduate Admissions Office, PO Box 48, Milton Keynes MK7 6AB.

**NEC** The National Extension College
18 Brooklands Avenue, Cambridge CB2 2HN.

**OC** The Open College
781 Wilmslow Road, Didsbury, Manchester M20 8RW.

**OCA** The Open College of the Arts
Barnsley, South Yorkshire S70 6TU.

**CACC** Council for the Accreditation of Correspondence Colleges
27 Marylebone Road, London NW1 5JS.

**UDACE** Unit for the Development of Adult Continuing Education
94B London Road, Leicester LE2 0QS.

**Reference books** *The Open Learning Directory 1992* (Pergamon Open Learning); *UDACE UK Directory 1992 of Educational Guidance Services for Adults* obtainable from National Institute of Adult Continuing Education (NIACE) 19B DeMontfort Street, Leicester LE1 7GE.

## Support organisations for prospective students

**Women Returners Network**
181–203 Euston Street, London NW1 2EP; tel 071-388 3111.

**National Bureau for Handicapped Students**
40 Brunswick Square, London WC1 1AZ.

**National Bureau for Students with Disabilities**
336 Brixton Road, London SW9 7AA; tel 071-274 0565.

**Royal National Institute for the Blind**
Student Support Service, 224 Great Portland Street, London W1N 6AA; tel 071-388 1266.

**UK Council for Overseas Student Affairs**
UKCOSA, 60 Westbourne Grove, London W2 5SH; tel 071-229 9268.

**World University Services (WUS), Refugee Education Advisory Service**
20 Compton Terrace, London N1 2UN; tel 071-226 6747.

**The British Council: National Academic Recognition Centre (NARIC)**
Deals with compatibility between UK and overseas qualifications. The UK Naric, The British Council, 10 Spring Gardens, London SW1A 2BN; tel 071-930 8466.

## Useful organisations for careers advice and development information

**CSU** **Central Services Unit**
Crawford House, Precinct Centre, Manchester M13 9EP. (Works with the Association of Graduate Careers and Advisory Services to provide careers information.)

**CRAC** **Careers Research and Advisory Centre**
Sheraton House, Castle Park, Cambridge CB3 0AX. Publications available through: Hobson's Press, Bateman Street, Cambridge CB2 1LZ.

**COIC** **Careers and Occupational Information Centre**
Moorfoot, Sheffield S1 4PQ.

**Reading Reference:** *What Do Graduates Do: A Guide to First Degree Graduates and Diplomates Leaving Universities, Polytechnics and Colleges*, Alun Jones, CRAC.

**Ongoing Contacts:**

**BFUW** **British Federation of University Women**
Crosby Hall, Cheyne Walk, Chelsea London SW3 5BA. (Overseas contact with women graduates and professionals.)

**BPW** **UK Federation of Business and Professional Women**
23 Ansdell Street, Kensington, London W8 5BN (Affiliated to the International Federation of Business and Professional Women.)

**National Federation of Self-Employed and Small Businesses**
32 St. Annes Road West, Lytham St. Annes, Fylde, Lancashire FY8 1NY.

**Alliance of Small Firms of Self-Employed People**
42 Vine Road, East Molesey, Surrey KT8 9LF.

# INDEX